Routledge Revivals

An Introduction to Criminology

This book, first published in 1936, provides an introduction to the various branches of criminology, including criminal psychology and criminology as an applied science. This title also provides an overview of some of the different criminological schools and theories. This book will be of interest to students of criminology and sociology.

An Introduction to Criminology

W. A. Bonger

Translated from the Dutch
by Emil van Loo

First published in 1936
by Methuen & Co.

This edition first published in 2015 by Routledge
2 Park Square, Milton Park, Abingdon, Oxon, OX14 4RN
and by Routledge
711 Third Avenue, New York, NY 10017

Routledge is an imprint of the Taylor & Francis Group, an informa business

© 1936 W. A. Bonger

All rights reserved. No part of this book may be reprinted or reproduced or utilised in any form or by any electronic, mechanical, or other means, now known or hereafter invented, including photocopying and recording, or in any information storage or retrieval system, without permission in writing from the publishers.

Publisher's Note
The publisher has gone to great lengths to ensure the quality of this reprint but points out that some imperfections in the original copies may be apparent.

Disclaimer
The publisher has made every effort to trace copyright holders and welcomes correspondence from those they have been unable to contact.

A Library of Congress record exists under LC control number: 37014045

ISBN 13: 978-1-138-91158-1 (hbk)
ISBN 13: 978-1-315-69253-1 (ebk)

AN INTRODUCTION TO CRIMINOLOGY

by

DR. W. A. BONGER

Translated from the Dutch by
EMIL VAN LOO

WITH 6 DIAGRAMS

METHUEN & CO. LTD. LONDON
96 Essex Street W.C.2

First published in 1936

PRINTED IN GREAT BRITAIN

FOREWORD

THIS book appeared about three years ago in the Dutch 'University Extension Library' (*Volksuniversiteitsbibliotheek*). The size of the works which are published in this series is the same for all; and it was therefore impossible to deal equally with the various branches of criminology, more especially criminal psychology, where I have confined myself to giving a historical survey. The short bibliography has now been brought up to date.

This Introduction is widely used in the Netherlands by students, lawyers, and all those who are interested in the terrible problem of crime. I hope this will also be the case in English-speaking countries, where there exists, as far as I am aware, no such succinct survey of the subject.

If the book is received by the critics as favourably as was my *Criminality and Economic Conditions* many years ago I shall be satisfied.

I wish to express my thanks to the translator, Mr. E. van Loo, for the good care which he has bestowed on my book.

W. A. BONGER

AMSTERDAM
April 1936

CONTENTS

CHAPTER		PAGE
	FOREWORD	V
I.	INTRODUCTORY	1
	1. Definitions.	
	2. The disadvantages of criminality to society	5
	3. The sub-sciences of criminology	7
	4. Methods and means at the disposal of criminology	9
	5. On determinism.	20
II.	THE PRE-HISTORY OF CRIMINOLOGY (PRE-CRIMINOLOGY)	26
	6. Antiquity.	
	7. The Middle Ages	27
	8. The beginning of modern history (sixteenth century)	28
	9. The eighteenth century until the French revolution	30
	i. The opposition to the existing criminal law and criminal jurisprudence.	
	ii. The social causes of crime.	
	iii. The anthropological causes of crime.	
	10. From the French revolution until the eighteen-thirties	37
	i. The changes in criminal law, criminal jurisprudence and punishment.	
	ii. The social causes of crime.	
	iii. The anthropological causes of crime.	
III.	THE STATISTICIAN-SOCIOLOGISTS	47
	11. Introductory.	
	12. Criminal statistics as a static method	49
	13. Criminal statistics as a dynamic method	53

CONTENTS

CHAPTER	PAGE
IV. THE ITALIAN (OR ANTHROPOLOGICAL) SCHOOL	56

    14. Introductory.
        i. The early history between the beginning of the eighteen-thirties and the eighteen-seventies.
        ii. The personalities and their work.

    15. The theory of Lombroso 60
        i. Introductory.
        ii. The anthropology of the criminal.
        iii. The atavistic hypothesis.
        iv. The pathological hypothesis.
        v. The criminal type.
        vi. Conclusion. The influence of Lombroso on criminal jurisprudence.

    16. The theory of Ferri 76

V. THE FRENCH (OR ENVIRONMENT) SCHOOL . . 78

    17. The French school in the restricted sense.

    18. The economic environment school . . . 81

    19. Some etiological results of criminal sociology . 83
        i. Neglect of children, etc.
        ii. Destitution.
        iii. Covetousness.
        iv. Sexual demoralization.
        v. Alcoholism.
        vi. Lack of culture.
        vii. War.

    20. Physical environment 106
        i. Economic criminality.
        ii. Sexual criminality.
        iii. Aggressive criminality.
        iv. Political criminality.

VI. THE BIO-SOCIOLOGICAL SCHOOL 117
    21. Critical examination 117
    22. The law of individual variations . . . 121

CONTENTS

CHAPTER		PAGE
VII.	THE SPIRITUALISTIC SCHOOL	127
	23. General outline	127
	24. Critique of the theory	128
	25. The causes of low criminality among the irreligious	133
VIII.	ON CRIMINAL PSYCHOLOGY	137
	26. On the history of criminal psychology	137
	i. The pre-history of criminal psychology.	
	ii. Criminal psychology between 1870 and 1900.	
	iii. Criminal psychology after 1900.	
	27. The psychology of the criminal in general	147
	28. The significance of the psychology of the criminal for criminology	149
IX.	CRIMINOLOGY AS AN APPLIED SCIENCE	153
	29. Criminal hygiene	153
	30. Criminal policy	155

APPENDIX:

I.	LIST OF CRIMINOLOGICAL CONGRESSES, SOCIETIES AND PERIODICALS	161
II.	BIBLIOGRAPHY	167
	INDEX	175

DIAGRAMS

		PAGE
I.	THEFT AND GRAIN-PRICES IN BAVARIA, 1835–61	54
II.	THEFT, WHOLESALE FOOD PRICES, AND WHOLESALE PRICES OF INDUSTRIAL PRODUCTS	92
III.	THE COURSE OF ECONOMIC CRIMINALITY IN GERMANY AND FRANCE FOR THE VARIOUS MONTHS OF THE YEAR	109
IV.	THE CURVE OF SEXUAL AND AGGRESSIVE CRIMINALITY IN FRANCE AND ENGLAND DURING THE MONTHS OF THE YEAR	112
V.	THE COURSE OF AGGRESSIVE CRIMINALITY IN GERMANY FOR THE VARIOUS MONTHS OF THE YEAR	114
VI.	THE LAW OF INDIVIDUAL VARIATIONS (BODILY HEIGHT OF BELGIAN RECRUITS)	122

CHAPTER I

INTRODUCTORY

I. DEFINITIONS

BY criminology we mean the science whose purpose is the study of the phenomenon called criminality, in its entire extent (this is theoretical or 'pure' criminology)[1] whilst side by side with this theoretical science, and founded upon its conclusions, we have what is called practical or applied criminology. Criminology is an inductive science which, like other inductive sciences, observes the facts with the greatest possible exactitude, and endeavours with the aid of available methods to trace the causes of the phenomena coming to its notice (etiology). *Vere scire est per causas scire*—as Bacon has already taught us.

The subject-matter, therefore, of the science of criminology is criminality, i.e. the crimes which are committed and the persons who commit them; the juridical aspect of the problem, i.e. the legal formulation of the various crimes being at best a matter of indirect interest to the criminologist.

It may be useful to state briefly what exactly is meant by crime. From the formal or legal point of view, a crime is an action on which the community (*in casu* the State) has set a punishment—a definition which, like most formal definitions, does not take us much further. Another angle, from which we penetrate further into the essence of the question, is the view that crime belongs to the category of immoral actions. The question which is often asked, whether crime, *per se*,

[1] Taking 'criminology' in its widest sense, the other so-called social-pathological phenomena, such as pauperism, illegitimacy, prostitution, alchoholism, and suicide, which are all interrelated, have largely the same or kindred causes, and partially occur in each other's etiology, also belong to the science of criminology. In this Introduction, however, these phenomena do not come under consideration.

It was the French anthropologist P. Topinard (1830–1911) who gave this science the name of criminology.

should always be ranked as immoral, must, I believe, be answered in the affirmative, although admittedly there are instances (i.e. under despotic rule) where an action stamped as criminal is not felt to be immoral by anybody. In that case we have to do with actions which are merely formally criminal. A penal code of that sort does not, of course, tend to ensure the protection of the community; on the contrary, it gives all the more cause for resistance to the despotic ruler. It must not be thought, however, that even in those cases where both factors of the definition are present, the whole of the population necessarily considers the action in question as immoral, or even to a uniform degree. In any complex form of society, where the population is divided into sharply differentiated groups and classes, and in which each person may belong to more than one group, differences of appreciation in these matters may be observed. We may, however, be justified in saying that in modern countries practically all actions which are qualified as crimes are felt to be immoral by the great majority of the people—albeit in different measure. Even the professional criminal thinks of theft as of something immoral —namely when it is committed to his own detriment, or to that of a member of his gang. It is almost superfluous to add that apart from the differences mentioned above, the degree of public disapprobation of all the countless prohibited actions varies very widely, and ranges from a minimum—as in cases of poaching or smuggling—to the height of moral indignation in some of the worst cases of manslaughter or murder.

If one asks oneself what actually constitutes the essence of an immoral action it becomes apparent that there are two sides to it: subjectively, i.e. from the individual's point of view, such actions go counter to moral sentiment; while objectively, i.e. from society's point of view, they constitute a danger to the interests of the community. Sociological (and, more especially, ethnological) research does not leave any doubt upon this point: the term 'immoral' means—from the standpoint of the community, 'anti-social'. Thus, the utilitarians erred when they imagined they could define morality as utility for the individual; but this view becomes correct when for the individual one substitutes the community; for the whole of our code of morals is designed for its benefit and protection. Man is extremely sensitive to that which might harm the community as a whole; and broadly speaking, this instinct has but rarely proved itself wrong (one instance of this being the persecution of witches). In such cases it was experience which acted as a corrective. In view of the absolute supremacy of society over the still growing and maturing individual the latter, as a rule, tends to accept without demur the moral code prevailing in his time.

An immoral action, therefore, is an anti-social action which is felt as such. *A priori*, one cannot speak of any action as being either immoral or criminal *per se*; there is, in fact, no such thing as a 'natural' offence. It all depends upon social conditions. Some actions, however, are so obviously hostile to the interests of any and every society that there was hardly ever a time when they were not prohibited, as in the case of theft, because of its parasitical character. Society is continually changing—and, especially in its present phase, very rapidly. Hence the great changes which take place in our conception of morality, and which are reflected also in criminal law. These, however, take time; and the tension between a rapidly-changing morality and a comparatively static criminal law can, at times, become very great.

Crimes belong to the immoral actions; but they only form part thereof. Generally speaking, one may say that they are the gravest; they form, as it were, the kernel, the grosser but fundamental part. One might compare moral and criminal laws, respectively, with two concentric circles, of which the former would be the larger. The difference in size between the two may vary considerably, according to time and place; sometimes the two circles cover each other completely, whereas at other times their circumferences lie far apart. In the former case this is a bad sign; any society which threatens with punishment almost every transgression is internally weak.

Our provisional conclusion is therefore that a crime is a serious anti-social action to which the State re-acts consciously. This reaction, as is already evident from our formal definition, consists of punishment.

The question finally remains: what is punishment?[1] The answer is that to punish is to inflict pain; but it is not here that its difference from the moral reaction to an immoral action is to be looked for, for the latter is also of a painful nature. It does not alter matters in the least that sensitivity to this pain varies enormously in different people, and is often very small indeed. The real difference lies in the fact that moral reprobation emanates from one or more individuals spontaneously; whereas punishment is a conscious action on the part of the collectivity (*in casu* the State). The content of a reproof is nothing but a moral condemnation; but when it is incorporated in criminal law, and pronounced by a judge, it becomes a punishment.

A similar demarcation is indicated in the other direction. Revenge, too, is pain caused intentionally, but it is an irrational reaction of the emotions, generally of an impulsive nature, on the part of one or more persons, to a wrong which they have suffered. Punishment, on the other hand, does not come from one or more persons; it is meted out by the group, the collectivity, acting consciously and rationally. Even in cases where nothing else is aimed at but the satisfaction of feelings of revenge, a new and essential element has emerged, i.e. conscious reaction emanating from the collectivity.

Punishment, however, did originate in revenge; and the latter has certainly played its part in ensuring the safety of the community—be it imperfectly, and accompanied by grave disadvantages. In primitive forms of society taking revenge is, indeed, morally imperative. Gradually, however, as the community begins to take over this function, the position is changed, and has now turned the other way round: it is

[1] To criminology also belongs penology, or the science of punishment. The limited size of the present volume prevents a thorough treatment of this subject. A few remarks made here, and in the last chapter, must suffice.

DEFINITIONS

revenge by the wronged party which is prohibited—not only morally, but in criminal law as well.

Present-day punishment contains two elements. Firstly, it serves—as it always has done—to satisfy the feelings of revenge and revulsion on the part of the members of the collectivity. No amount of theorizing about 'returning evil with evil', etc., however ingeniously invented, can alter this in the least. But this element, which was at one time supreme, suffered an important check from the second.

This second element is the safeguarding of the community (*la défense sociale*). To some extent it has always been present—if only in a more or less unconscious form. It has, however, now entered into the social consciousness, and is already of considerable importance. Society takes certain measures against its harmful members, one of the chief of which is, surely, the attempt to educate them with a view to fitting them once more for social life. Punishment—i.e. the pain which it is intended to inflict—also belongs to society's armoury; but the difference between educative and correctional 'measures' and punishment is not nearly so great as many theoretical criminologists would have us believe. The pain inflicted by these measures is usually also of a serious nature, for it implies robbing the subject of his or her freedom; it does not, therefore, differ so very much.

To sum up, our conclusion is that *crime is a serious antisocial action to which the State re-acts consciously, by inflicting pain (either punishment or correctional measures)*.

2. THE DISADVANTAGES OF CRIMINALITY TO SOCIETY

We have to do, indeed, with an extensive and deeply-rooted social disease, which has dug itself into the very body of society like a kind of ulcer; at times even threatening its very existence, but always harmful in the highest degree. Countless crimes are committed, and millions of criminals condemned, every year. *Economically*, the disadvantages to society are very great. For the United States of America various estimates have been made. Thus, Schlapp and Smith, in their book *The New Criminology* (1928) arrive at a figure of four milliards of dollars ($4,000,000,000) per year in respect of direct damages, and between five and six milliards indirect losses (loss of production power, cost of police, etc.), in all between nine and ten milliards a year.[1] Other estimates are still higher.[2] I have no means of judging the reliability of these estimates, neither am I in a position to form an estimate, on the same lines, for other countries; but I think it is undeniable that crime is a source of stupendous waste of money to society. Next to the economic, we have, moreover, the still more important *moral* disadvantages. If criminality is closely bound up with the moral standards of a people, in return it sends out demoralizing influences towards the normal sections of the population. And when one adds to all this the damage and grief suffered by the victims of the crime, and also the constant menace which criminality constitutes to society, the total obtained is already a formidable one. Neither ought we to forget the suffering on the part of the criminal himself, who—in whatever way one may wish to judge him, is after all, a part of humanity too. Superficially-judging people sometimes try to represent the criminal classes as always playing a winning hand in their war on the community, leading quite a pleasant life on the proceeds of their booty. This may be so in an isolated case here and there; but sooner or later—generally sooner—they lose the fight, and then the hand of society presses on them heavily indeed. If ever the words of Goethe: 'Der Menschheit ganze Jammer fasst mich an' were applicable, it is when one views the phenomenon of criminality in its entire range and depth.[3]

The reasons for the study of criminology should therefore be clear. Admittedly it is a science which is widely studied for

[1] *Vide* p. 50 et seq.
[2] *Vide* also, e.g. Brasol, *The Elements of Crime* (1927). p. 75 et seq. L. F. Bower, in his *The Economic Waste of Sin* (1924) also gives some estimates for the other social-pathological phenomena.
[3] Mueller-Lyer, in his monumental and far too little-known work *Soziologie der Leiden* (1914) looks upon this form of suffering as a highly important part of the whole.

DISADVANTAGES OF CRIMINALITY

its own sake, just like other sciences; crime and criminals are not a bit less interesting than stars or microbes. The element of *la science pour la science* should be present in every scientist, otherwise he will be no good in his profession; and this applies to the criminologist too. But this point of view is secondary as compared with the practical aspect, just as in the case of medical science. Indeed, comparison with the latter repeatedly suggests itself. Criminology ought before anything to show humanity the way to combat, and especially, prevent, crime. 'Savoir pour prévoir' (Comte). What is required more than anything is sound knowledge, whereas up to the present we have had far too much of dogma and dillettantism. Whoever is in close touch with what is called socio-pathological phenomena should make a note of this—especially criminal jurists, whose knowledge of the law imperatively needs to be supplemented with that of the subject-matter with which it has to deal.

3. THE SUB-SCIENCES OF CRIMINOLOGY

Criminology is a complex science. It consists of:

(i) *Criminal anthropology*, i.e. the science of criminal man (somatic), a section of natural science; anthropology being sometimes called 'the last chapter of zoology'. It attempts to answer such questions as: what peculiar bodily characteristics has the criminal? What relation is there between race and criminality? etc.

(ii) *Criminal sociology*, i.e. the science of criminality as a social phenomenon. Its principal concern is, therefore, to find out to what extent the causes of criminality have their origin in society (social etiology). In a wider sense, the study of physical (geographical, climatological, and meteorological) environment forms also a part of this sub-section.

(iii) *Criminal psychology*, i.e. the science of psychological phenomena in the field of crime. The chief subject-matter of its study is the psychology of the criminal, e.g. to what type or types he belongs; further, differentiation according to sex, age and race; and finally, collective or crowd-criminality.

Further, what may be termed the 'psychology of crime' (motives and checks) belongs to this section. Lastly, the psychology of the other persons *in foro* (witnesses, judge, counsel, etc.), and the psychology of the confession.

(iv) *Criminal psycho- and neuro-pathology*, i.e. the science of the psychopathic or neurotic criminal.

(v) *Penology*, i.e. the science of the origin and development of punishment, its significance and utility.

These five sections together constitute theoretical or 'pure' criminology (*reine Wissenschaft*). Founded on these, we have, further:

(vi) *Applied criminology*, i.e. criminal hygiene and criminal policy.

Taking the conception of the science of criminology in its widest sense, we should also include in it:

(vii) *Criminalistics* (*police scientifique*)—an applied science whose purpose is to trace the technique of crime and its detection. It is a combination of the psychology of crime and the criminal, and of chemistry, physics, knowledge of goods and materials, graphology, etc.

The present work will treat chiefly of the history of criminology; the various schools (sub. i and ii) will be outlined, a few brief remarks only will be made on the subject of criminal psychology (sub. iii), while certain conclusions concerning applied criminology will form the finish.[1] The limited space available in this little book will then have been filled. The author, moreover, is not in a position to write authoritatively either on psycho- and neuro-pathology,[2] or criminalistics,[3]

---

[1] About this, for a more extensive treatment, *vide*, e.g. D. Simons, *Problemen van het Strafrecht* (1929), (*Problems of Criminal Law*) Par. iii.

[2] For this department of the science I refer the reader to the excellent work by H. van der Hoeven, *Psychiatrie: een handleiding voor juristen en maatschappelijke werkers* (*Psychiatrics: a manual for jurists and social workers*) (2nd impression, 1928–1930), and K. Birnbaum, *Die psychopathischen Verbrecher* (2nd edition, 1926), and *Kriminalpsychopathologie und Psycho-pathologische Verbrecher Kunde* (2nd edition, 1931).

[3] The first scientific student of criminalistics was Hans Gross, *Handbuch für Untersuchungsrichter als System der Kriminalistik*, 1st

METHODS OF CRIMINOLOGY

both of which are legitimate fields of study for specialists only.

4. THE METHODS AND MEANS AT THE DISPOSAL OF CRIMINOLOGY

are similar to those of other inductive sciences. They were first applied in physics, and were later adopted by sociology and psychology. In one respect we shall, in the science with which we are dealing here, always be in an unfavourable position as compared with physics: this is due to the quasi-impossibility of experimentation. A few pseudo-experiments, made here and there, can never fill this enormous void.

The first step, just as in other similar sciences, is *to collect the facts* (after the example of sociography, one might call this part *'criminography'*). The conditions to be fulfilled by explorers in this field are no different from those in other sciences (honesty, objectivity, critical sense, etc.); while, just as in all sciences dealing with *genus homo sapiens*, interest and sympathy for human beings as such are essential; one must feel the urge to serve suffering humanity by one's knowledge. An inhuman criminologist is quite as great an absurdity as an inhuman surgeon.

How are the facts obtained? Here, a distinction must be made between criminal sociology on the one hand, and criminal anthropology and psychology on the other.

The principal source of factual material for the first-named branch is *criminal statistics*. With the aid of this method of registering criminality one can get a bird's-eye-view, in figures, of the whole phenomenon. To France must be accorded the great merit of having inaugurated this work (1826)—apart

edition, 1893, 6th edition, 1914). I would further mention W. Stieber, *Praktisches Lehrbuch der Kriminalpolizei*, 2e Auflage, herausgegeben von H. Schneickert (1921), Niceforo-Lindenau, *Die Kriminalpolizei und ihre Hilfswissenschaften* (1909), and *Kriminal taktik und Kriminaltechnik* (4th edition, 1933), Reiss, *Manuel de police scientifique* (1911), R. Heindl, *System und Praxis der Daktyloskopie und der sonstigen technischen Methoden der Kriminalpolizei* (1921, 3rd edition, 1927), and E. Locard, *Traité de criminalistique*, (1931).

from some earlier attempts, as, for example, in England (1805). Baden (1834), Belgium (1835), Bavaria (1835), Austria (1852), Prussia (1854), England (1857), Germany (1882), and the Netherlands (1896), followed suit. As far as I am aware all modern states, with the exception of U.S.A., have now got this expedient at their disposal.

Criminal statistics originated in judicial statistics—in which the number of cases dealt with, acquittals, dismissed cases, appeals, etc., are listed. Both are now quite separate and independent, and serve different ends. The unit of criminal statistics is no longer the crime or the accused, but the condemned person. Some statistics, such as the English Criminal Statistics, also give the number of 'crimes known to the police'. Besides in the statistics of crime, certain data which may be important to criminology may sometimes be found in prison statistics. In the Netherlands, moreover, there exists a special publication dealing with criminality among children and young persons, namely: *de Statistiek van de toepassing der Kinderwetten* (*Statistics concerning the application of Child Laws*).

What fields do present-day criminal statistics cover?

Whereas, in the first years of their existence, only total figures were given roughly grouped according to crimes against persons, property and the State—which division is by itself not very informative in criminological research—they now state (1) all the crimes separately, generally in order of sequence, as they are numbered according to the code of criminal law. From a criminological point of view, this method is also imperfect for some classes of offence, as the same offence may be committed from entirely different motives. Arson, for instance, may originate in revenge, in which case it belongs to aggressive criminality (together with, for instance, cruelty, damaging of property, etc.)—but also from economic motives, when it is ranged with fraud and suchlike. This, however, is a statistical imperfection which it would be difficult to remove. Next to the offence stated comes (2) the *locus delicti* (county, large or small town, etc.). As regards the

METHODS OF CRIMINOLOGY

person of the condemned the unit adopted is the condemned without appeal, i.e. the criminal to whom the usual legal facilities are no longer accessible. In the Netherlands, and also in Belgium, a person sentenced more than once in the same year is counted only once; in other countries as many times as he is sentenced. In 1896 the latter method of counting was also employed in the Netherlands, but this was changed some years after without, however, altering the aspect of the matter in any significant degree, but meanwhile breaking the continuity. Since 1911 both sets of figures are given.

Further data are: (3) sex, (4) age, (5) civil status, (6) legitimacy, (7) trade or profession, (8) economic circumstances, (9) religion, (10) degree of education, (11) alcoholism, if any, (12) migration, (13) recidivism, if any, (14) punishments, if any. Criminal statistics, however, do not by a long way supply information concerning all these points.[1] In the Netherlands, for example, those mentioned under (8) are lacking;[2] in other countries, however, many more.

These statistics relate, of course, to those criminals who are sentenced irrevocably (i.e. without appeal) during the year stated. As a certain number of them, however, committed their crime during the preceding calendar year, the statistics of criminality do not quite coincide with the actual crimes committed in a given year. The statistics 'limp behind', as it were; a thing which ought not to be lost sight of if one wishes to relate the curve of criminality to other social facts.

[1] The German *Kriminalstatistik für das Jahr 1927* (Reimar Hobbing, Berlin, 1930), gives a synopsis for 33 countries, in which one gets a bird's eye view of all data provided by criminal statistics.

[2] In order to avoid misunderstanding, attention is here drawn to the fact that not nearly all the Dutch data are published. Since 1911, personalia are no longer to be found regularly in the statistics; those for 1911-15 are published in a separate volume, and for 1919 they also exist. In 1929, data concerning sex, age, and civil status are given again. For the years 1913, 1914, 1915, 1920, 1921, and 1922, no tables appeared; while the volumes 1923 and 1924 did not appear at all. For 1926, only an introduction appeared, which also gave a few data from 1923 and 1924. Since 1926, an introduction has been published again, with tables, but in abbreviated form.

The tables are available, and may be searched by interested persons at the Central Bureau for Statistics at The Hague.

The statistics of 'crimes known to the police' do not suffer from this shortcoming.

Criminal statistics have sometimes been severally criticized. To some extent this was the same kind of criticism which is always levied at any sort of statistics. There are always people with minds too vague to understand the meaning of figures; while others get discouraged because statistics are a difficult method of study, and not a short cut for any layman to arrive at great truths without any trouble. It cannot be denied, moreover, that statistics have been very grossly abused—for which, however, only the abusers can be blamed. It was no doubt this kind of critic who invented the witticism: 'first we get lies, then big lies, and after that—statistics'. This amiability might well be repaid in the same coin: first we have fools, then silly fools, and after that, people who do not understand figures! Goethe knew better: 'Man sagt oft: Zahlen regieren die Welt. Das aber ist gewiss: Zahlen zeigen wie sie regiert wird.'

One special objection might, however, be made to criminal statistics, and that is their incompleteness. And, indeed, nobody can deny the truth of this assertion. Even the records of crimes known to the police, which in some countries are kept up to date, and which keep nearer than anything to the actual facts, are not complete. Numerous smaller offences are not even noticed by the injured party; and of those which are, a good many are never notified to the police. There are many different reasons for this. It may be that the injured party does not consider the matter sufficiently important (quite small thefts, insults, very slight assaults, etc.); or that he does not want to be bothered with having to appear in a criminal court; or, again, he may refrain from prosecuting out of pity for the criminal or his family, etc. Further, out of the total number of crimes which are notified, a certain proportion are not followed up by the authorities because of their unimportance; or, maybe, the offender is discharged with a caution; while in other cases prosecution is impossible because the offender cannot be traced. Finally, only a certain number out of the persons who are prosecuted is included in the

METHODS OF CRIMINOLOGY 13

statistics, the others being either acquitted or discharged. Nevertheless, however great the discrepancy may be between the number of offences actually committed and the number of persons sentenced *in respect of those offences*, it would be quite incorrect to say that the number of criminals who in the long run manage to escape the arm of the law is at all considerable. Often—indeed, generally—they repeat their crimes, and sooner or later—usually sooner—they are called to account for one of them. Even professional criminals, the most intelligent and persistent category, do not usually remain at large for long, and the number of their crimes which then comes to light is generally large.

Is, then, this admitted incompleteness of criminal statistics (incomplete, that is to say, chiefly as regards the crimes committed in any given year) sufficient justification for declaring statistics useless in scientific research? Not in the least. In some branches of science, e.g. demography, and in some sections of economic statistics, the available statistical material is quite complete, and this completeness is, for those branches, highly desirable, and, indeed, necessary. As soon, however, as one starts to use statistics as a method for etiological research, completeness of material is no longer essential; it may, indeed, be mere ballast. What is chiefly required in this matter is for the material to be sufficiently representative, so that one is able to say whether the relative proportion of the known and the unknown facts is a fairly constant one (*pars pro toto*). For a long time this principle has been put into practice in commerce, e.g. in 'sampling' parcels of goods, and it is now admitted to be correct in statistical theory. Other similar branches, such as, for instance, medical statistics, follow the same procedure. When the results of experiments in, say, 1,000 cases of typhoid are published, nobody in his senses would quarrel with the conclusions on the grounds that not all sufferers from typhoid were examined.

As regards the question of whether the figures of criminal statistics are sufficiently representative, there cannot be any doubt. Hardly any statistics of a comparable nature have such complete data at their disposal. The only thing we should make sure of is that the figures *themselves* are not inadequate; in other words, that chance is excluded. And this is much more likely to be the case than laymen—and sometimes even experts—might imagine. As evidence of this I recall an example which I have also mentioned elsewhere: out of a number of 1,260 criminals, 576, or forty-five per cent, belonged to a particular category (*in casu* catholics), whereas the figure of thirty-five per cent was 'expected'. During a discussion it was asserted that this might be merely chance; in other words, that the figures were of no importance. As a matter of fact, the chance that this was merely accidental is

$$\frac{1}{60,000,000,000,000}$$

i.e. one out of 30,000 times the earth's population!

When read critically and used expertly, therefore, criminal statistics are, without the slightest doubt, an excellent aid to criminal research. One has, however, to be careful in making *international comparisons*. The differences in law, jurisprudence, the administration of justice (e.g. the use or otherwise, by the Public Prosecutor, of the prerogative of prosecution), police organization, etc., are so great that one would not be justified in drawing any conclusions in regard to actual differences in criminality, and even less in regard to the moral standards of the population. Only in those cases when there can be next to no divergence in the formulation of the offence, when the general degree of public reprobation is about the same (as in the case of murder), and when, after that, the figures differ considerably, these data may be significant.

Criminal statistics, based as they are, on the counting of elementary facts, supply information concerning criminality as a mass-phenomenon. They let us down, however, as soon as facts are asked for which cannot be ascertained by counting, but only by investigation. To name only one instance: the criminal's educational standard, or his environment, can only be got at by such an investigation. Next to statistics, therefore, we have to employ the method of inquiry. This may be

METHODS OF CRIMINOLOGY 15

done either *officially* (i.e. taken in hand by the organs of justice themselves), or *unofficially* (i.e. undertaken by private investigators).

The available official material has of late years continually improved, and looks like getting better still, as time goes on. This is due to changes which take place in jurisprudence. The judge of the early days did not have to bother himself overmuch about the person of the delinquent. If the latter was found guilty, all the judge had to do was to mete out a certain quantity of punishment, without respect of person. Under the influence of the science of criminology, however, this has altogether changed, punishment with a definite aim gradually coming to the fore. Nowadays the judge has at his disposal a whole arsenal of punishments and correctional measures from which to make a suitable selection. In order to do this successfully he has to be well acquainted with the person of the criminal. He therefore causes an inquiry to be made by official or semi-official investigators. In some countries this inquiry is obligatory; in Belgium, for instance, every more or less serious delinquent is examined anthropologically, psychologically, and sociologically (e.g. as to the environment from which he hails). In the Netherlands this is not obligatory, but the number of inquiries is steadily increasing. This method was first put into practice—as, indeed, often happens—in juvenile law. The Netherlands personal criminal records, which were introduced recently, serve, amongst other things, to collect these and similar data. The results of these inquiries contain rich scientific material, which is not being used nearly enough.

We now come to the investigations which are conducted by private people. As early as the eighteenth century, F. G. De Pitaval started a collection of 'interesting cases', *Causes célèbres et intéressantes* (1734 et seq.), followed in Germany by Häring and Hitzig in *Der neue Pitaval* (1842–91), and still later by *Der Pitaval der Gegenwart* (1903 et seq.). In 1808 and 1811, the celebrated criminal jurist Anselm von Feuerbach published his book *Merkwürdige Kriminalrechtsfälle*—perhaps the best of its kind written. In 1881, A. Bataille commenced the publication of his *Causes criminelles et mondaines*. Many other works of this kind might be mentioned. Prison warders, prison clergymen, etc., who in the course of their function came into contact with criminals, have also contributed, by the publication of their memoirs, to the material at the disposal of criminology; amongst these are the Abbé Faure, in his *Souvenir de la Roquette*, and G. Moreau, in his *Souvenirs de la Petite et de la Grande Roquette*.

It cannot be denied that works of this kind (they cannot, strictly speaking, be called 'investigations'), may have a certain value for criminology; but they also have very serious defects. From their very titles it is evident that they are often more sensational than anything else, and the interest with which they are read is usually not entirely of the scientific variety. They invariably relate, moreover, to a very special kind of crime and criminal—the kind which occurs only rarely. The 'ordinary' crime and criminal—among whom, after all, we find many serious cases—are hardly, if ever, dealt with by them; and these are surely the most important to the student of criminology.

In this field, too, improvement has been effected lately. Well-trained criminologists have invaded this field of study and begun to investigate 'ordinary' cases, both personally and with the aid of official data. Pioneering work in this field was done in Holland (I hardly know anything in foreign literature to rank with this work) by N. Muller's *Biographisch aetiologisch onderzoek over recidive bij misdadigers tegen den eigendom* (1908) (*Biographical etiological inquiry into recidivism of offenders against property*). This was followed by others, e.g. Dr. H. Hillesum's *Biographisch onderzoek naar de werking van het Rijksopvoedingsgesticht voor meisjes en naar de oorzaken der meisjesmisdadigheid* (1918) (*Biographical inquiry into the working of the State Reformatory School for Girls and into the causes of criminality among girls*); Dr. S. J. Meyers' *Rijksopvoedingsgestichten, meer in het bijzonder dat voor meisjes en de resultaten daar verkregen* (1918) (*State Reformatory Schools, more especially* those for Girls, and the results obtained therein); Dr. S. van Mesdag: *Ontucht door onderwijzers* (*Offences against morality by teachers*) (*Tijdschrift voor Strafrecht XXXII*, 1922), and Dr. W. Schenk: *Wangedrag van kinderen* (1935) (*Misbehaviour of children*). It is this kind of research of which criminology stands in the greatest need and it is therefore to be hoped that the above works will be followed by many others.

Criminal statistics and investigation are the chief sources of material which criminal sociology employs. In addition to these, however, we should mention the autobiography—which is very rare (criminals not being, as a rule, great writers). A good example of criminal autobiography is to be found in the memoirs of the Roumanian master-swindler Manulescu. R. Hesse has also collected similar material in his *Les Criminels peints par eux-mêmes* (1912).

Dr. Muller, in his earlier-mentioned work, quotes at length from some autobiographies. It need not be said that these data should be regarded with a critical eye indeed. Art, too (especially the sociological novel), may be of importance to criminology. Ferri pointed this out at length in his *I delinquenti nell' arte* (1896). In the well-known controversy as to whether this is true for sociology in general I place myself unreservedly on the side of those who answer the question in the affirmative, but only in the sense that art can serve science *indirectly*, by putting the investigator on the track of finding out the truth. For the artist seeks Beauty, and we should not require of him always to serve Truth as well—not even the writer of the so-called 'naturalistic' novel. No man of science, therefore, should go exclusively by what he finds stated as a fact, in a work of art; while on the other hand, it would be utter foolishness not to avail oneself of what artists with a sociological trend, such as Balzac and Zola, with their great knowledge and intuition, have bequeathed to humanity.

Finally, I would draw attention to the value for criminology of personal observation. Laboratory investigators who are out of touch with life are quite unfit for the work, and the same may even be said of anthropologists of the same class.

It is also useful to keep posted about the crimes reported in the newspapers day by day. The well-known Prosper Despine used to get his material largely from reliable newspaper reports. Unfortunately, the Press of to-day strives after sensation more than anything, as a result of which newspaper reports have lost much of their value and reliability.

With regard to the methods of investigation used by *criminal anthropology* we need not dwell upon these here; they are the same as those of the ordinary somatic anthropology. The criminal's bodily measures are taken during his stay in prison, the strength of his muscles is examined, the sharpness of his eyesight tested, etc., etc.

As regards *criminal psychology*, we base ourselves, as we do to some extent in criminal sociology, on the facts as they are shown in the records of criminal cases, etc. The Dutch psychologist Heymans calls this the biographical method. I have already mentioned before the objections to this method. In this field, however, great improvements have also been made. The individual records contain increasingly more psychological information. Well-schooled psycho-criminologists have set themselves the task of describing, with the aid of these records, as well as personal investigation, various categories of 'ordinary' criminals.

In those departments of the science with which we have dealt above, the point of departure—in contradistinction from criminal statistics, where the counting of numbers is the sole method used—is investigation. As soon, however, as these investigations assume a somewhat extensive character and begin to yield a mass of facts, the results are again worked out in statistical figures. There is, therefore, no essential difference between the two methods.

As soon as sufficient facts have been collected which can stand the test of criticism, the really scientific work begins. Although the collecting of facts pre-supposes a certain scientific insight, the material itself is both blind and mute. It has to be manipulated, split up into its component parts,

METHODS OF CRIMINOLOGY

isolated, and finally grouped according to constantly common features. After that the etiological labour can commence, that is to say, tracing causes of events: that which preceded in time and was close by in space; and the presentation of these elements, as factors in the case and, if possible, in a percentage.

The method used by criminology is the same which is used in other inductive sciences; i.e. the method of comparison. Just as in mathematics one tries to deduct unknown factors from known ones. In doing this one may proceed either *statically* or *dynamically* (to use the terminology of Auguste Comte).

In the static method the facts are thought of as immobile, and situations are compared with each other as they appear at a given moment. We may, for instance, try to find out the cause of a certain type of crime, e.g. the aggressive (assaults, etc.); and in doing so we find that this differs considerably in different parts of any country (or, maybe, in two different countries). We must then find out whether there are any other social facts which show a great difference in these parts respectively. If this is found to be the case then we consider whether some relation cannot be traced between these two parallel divergencies (in this case, for instance, consumption of alcohol may differ). Should this be so, then we are on the track of the cause of the difference, and, with that, of the phenomenon itself. In the same way one can set to work, not only geographically, but in a general sociological sense. When, for instance, a considerable difference in a given type of criminality is observed in different classes (e.g. in economic crime such as theft, etc.), one seeks to ascertain whether this can be explained by reason of the difference in the criminal's social position. Psychologically, this method is, as a matter of fact, the one most generally used. For instance, it may be observed that a given psychological type appears in a given type of crime with a certain frequency, whereupon one inquires whether this frequency is either greater or less than it is in non-criminal 'human material'. From this, either a positive or negative pre-disposition of the type may be deduced.

The dynamic or kinetic method follows the facts as they move along. To take the same example: having ascertained that there has been a decrease in aggressive criminality in the course of time, one should then inquire whether there has been any other social fact which has also undergone a change during the same period. If this is so, one may suspect (in the case of fluctuating facts even more strongly) that there is some relation between the two series. This relation is often expressed in more precise terms with the aid of mathesis (calculation of the co-efficient of correlation). The nature of this relation cannot, however, be indicated by this method. Series A may be dependent upon series B; but it may also be the other way round, while it is also quite feasible that they have no mutual causal relation at all, but are both governed by a third series, C. The point where causality is to be found may then become apparent from another angle; e.g. by comparison of the times of occurrence (which of the two happened first), or by reasoning along psychological lines. In sociology the dynamic method is usually preferred to the static, isolation of the relevant factor being easier that way. In a complex form of society this is often difficult by the static method.

When a causal relation has been discovered, no matter how, it will be necessary to get the newly found provisional truth confirmed by other methods. If this confirmation is obtained on all sides, one ascends from the plane of hypothesis towards that of certitude, and the elements of a law make their appearance. The investigator in this field should, however, put out of his mind the illusion that this class of law can ever rank in dependability with, for instance, laws of nature.

5. ON DETERMINISM
(*'N'est pas criminel qui veut'*)

A book of this kind on an inductive science is, of course, not the right place for philosophical reflections. Inductive sciences are not based upon philosophy. It would be a bad look-out for them if they were, because the greatest differences of opinion prevail, among philosophers, concerning the most fundamental problems of their science. As the natural sciences prove, one can be an excellent student of an inductive science without having the slightest notion of philosophy. The same is true of sociology in general, and of criminology in particular. Philosophy stands at the top, not at the base of the sciences.

It cannot be denied, however, that in the sciences which are concerned with Man and Society, there is one problem of philosophy which refuses to be ignored, and that is the question of determinism. If the will of man is free, i.e. causeless,[1] then there is no point in looking for its causes. We refrain from discussing the matter here—it has been discussed to death. Indeterminism counts its most powerful opponents among philosophers themselves; the line runs from Democritus, over Spinoza, Leibnitz, Hume, Schopenhauer, down to Heymans. He who, nevertheless, still adheres to the doctrine of free will, cannot be admitted to the criminologist fraternity. An indeterminist criminologist is a living *contradictio in adjecto*. On the other hand, criminology itself has contributed the clearest proofs of the rightness of the determinist standpoint.

Although, therefore, there is no special reason for me to deal with the question in these pages, I will permit myself one or two remarks, chiefly of a practical nature. In the first place, how is it possible that so many people, notwithstanding the closest reasoning and the most convincing facts (one need only think of the significant fact that suicide, the only *deliberate* death, is among the most constant causes of death), and although every indeterminist is, in practical life, a determinist, still persist in adhering to the doctrine of free will?

The deepest ground for the doctrine of free will is the fact that Man hardly, if at all, understands the causes which determine his will.[2] Man *feels* free in his 'willing'—either wholly or partly. With a conceit only equalled by lack of

[1] The terminology according to which man's free will is the cause of his actions, is, of course, absurd.

[2] Spinoza: . . . 'homines se liberos esse opinentur, quandoquidem suarum volitionum suique appetitus sunt conscii, et de causis, a

logic, the conclusion is jumped at that causes do not, therefore, exist; but it is forgotten that by investigating the cases of *other people* it is possible to discover the causes in question—which also apply to the person himself. This feeling of freedom has, like so many others, become petrified into a dogma—with the aid of a certain amount of logic of a sort. And dogmas—we know it by experience—have a long life!

But it is not here that the sole reason is to be found for the persistence with which the doctrine of free will is adhered to; for, as a matter of fact, even non-dogmatically inclined people believe in it nowadays. More probably the reason lies in the fear that, without free will, morality would lose its foundation; that there would be an end to responsibility; that punishment would no longer be possible; in short, *finis mundi*! This view has been expressly stated by a number of authors, and one may hear it stated every day. 'We postulate indeterminism in the interests of the reality of our moral life,' the pragmatist James has said somewhere.[1] This sort of reasoning has, of course, nothing whatever to do with science. It is in the same street with that of a geologist who 'postulates', in the interests of humanity, that there must be no more earthquakes! Then there is, of course, the much larger group in whom this fear plays some part in their sub-conscious, and so prevents them from taking notice of the very strong arguments against their views.

Should this fear be well-founded, then even the most hard-boiled determinist would have to admit that the case is a serious one. It is, however, entirely unfounded. There are countless convinced determinists who, in everybody's opinion, are good and upright people, and who feel just as much responsible for their actions as others do; who feel guilty and repentant (though they may, perhaps, call these feelings by somewhat different names), when they have failed in any respect, etc., and who would not think it immoral or absurd

quibus disponuntur ad appetendum et volendum, quia earum sunt ignari, ne per somnium cogitant' (*Ethica* I, appendix).

[1] *Vide* C. J. Wijnaendts Francken, *Het vraagstuk van den vrijen wil* (1912) (*The Problem of the free will*), p. 74.

to be punished if they behaved wrongly. Even if the number of determinists of naturally weaker convictions were to increase greatly, this would not endanger society in any way.[1] Determinism would, indeed, be a very dangerous thing, if it taught us that 'nobody is responsible for his actions, let everybody do as he likes'. It is a regrettable fact that some determinists are not quite undeserving of this accusation. The beautifully-sounding, but actually absurd phrase 'to know all is to forgive all' has done more damage in this respect than I should care to say. On the contrary, however, determinism teaches us that every human being, without exception, is to be held accountable for his actions; not on the grounds of an imaginary free will, but because of the fact that he is a member of society, and that this society must take measures to protect itself from those who transgress its regulations, and so damage its interests. The still, small voice which tells man that some action he has committed is wrong, and which tells him to refrain from doing that kind of thing in future is, in reality, the voice of society.

Responsibility according to determinism, moreover, goes much further than according to indeterminism. This is quite obvious in the case of the responsibility of lunatics and psychopathics for crimes committed by them. Until the beginning of the nineteenth century they were punished equally with people of sound mind; lunatics too, it was thought, had a free will, and could very well act otherwise, if they only tried! In the name of this dogma they were ill-treated frightfully. At the end of the eighteenth century, however, when the science of psychiatrics was founded, views concerning criminal lunatics changed. From that time they were recognized as being diseased, and as such put beyond the reach of the law; they could not help being ill, after all. However great this improvement might be for science, as well as for mankind

[1] To him, who might say: 'I can't help what I have done wrong, and may, therefore, go scot-free,' one may reply, on the same level: 'Neither can society help punishing you.' It is told of Zeno that he replied to a thieving slave, whom he had punished, and who said that he was fated to steal: 'but also to be whipped!'

as a whole, dogma once again played its fatal part. This time the result was that these patients, among whom were some of the most dangerous criminals, often remained in society or returned there as free citizens. In the end, however, this part of the dogma, too, succumbed to criticism; henceforth lunatics were held responsible by society for their actions. The rest of the dogma is, of course, also bound to go by the board, as all dogmas do in the long run, although we have no particular reason for being optimistic concerning the brevity of their lifetime.

Theoretically, the difference between determinism and indeterminism is very great; practically, however, it is much smaller, and is continually getting smaller still. The number of indeterminists is decreasing, and in so far as they do adhere to their point of view, their conviction is weakening—absolute indeterminists do not any longer exist. On the other hand, determinism is not fatalism, but an Eastern exaggeration of a true Western thought. According to determinist conceptions a man is something more than a plaything of circumstances, a will-less being; he is a link in the shaping of events; and, indeed, by virtue of his qualities, a most important one. He is the possessor of a will which can be influenced, and indeed this fact is the basis of punishment. If the will could not be influenced by punishment, then punishment would be mere cruelty—as Hume has already remarked.[1]

The practical result of determinism, therefore, is not that all reaction against crime should disappear—a conclusion which indeterminists love to attribute to their opponents. The result of this would be, indeed, that humanity would be delivered helplessly into the power of its worst specimens. All it strives after is to remove the purposelessness—pain for the sake of pain—from the reaction, and to retain as its sole purpose: to be the greatest possible safeguard for society, consistent with the smallest possible amount of suffering

[1] In my opinion, indeterminism is the philosophical accompaniment of revenge. It is outside my present scope to go into this aspect further.

caused to the criminal. The opinion that determinists ought, to be consistent, to put all men on an equal footing, is an absurdity. Their feelings, too, are entirely in moral sympathy with the *homo nobilis*, and antipathetic to the *grand criminel*. The fact that neither of these two categories of mankind is what it is out of its own free will does not alter this in the least.

There is another important reason why determinists and indeterminists do not, in practice, stand so far apart as theory would lead us to suspect. According to determinist views everything which lies in the past was determined causally. But this also applies to the future. Notwithstanding the fact, however, that science is able correctly to state certain facts about the future, and that this power is sure to increase as time goes on—*scimus nonnulla, plura sciemus*—this must in the nature of things always be limited to the broad outline of events. This applies especially to those sciences whose purpose is the study of man and therefore especially to criminology. As the factors determining the fate of even a single human being are very numerous both from the point of view of propensities and from that of environment, it is unthinkable that they should become known to a sufficiently exact degree to foretell his future with any degree of certainty. According to the mathematics of probability it is possible to foretell, within fairly narrow limits, the result, either of *one* throw of *many* dice, or of *many* throws of a *single* die; but not the result of a *single* throw of a *single* die. Criminology will never succeed in foretelling the future fate—*in bonam aut in malam partem*—of the individuals which constitute its subject-matter, any more than the science of medicine, no matter how far it may yet develop, will be able to fix correctly the duration of each person's life. Determinists, too, know very well that the future contains much that is uncertain—fortunately, we might add—however certain it might be objectively.

CHAPTER II

THE PRE-HISTORY OF CRIMINOLOGY (PRE-CRIMINOLOGY)

CRIMINOLOGY is, in common with various other sciences, a child of the nineteenth century. Its beginnings date from about 1830, the same period as that in which sociology began its career. Criminology has, however, had its precursors, and they will be dealt with in the present chapter.[1] Properly speaking, there are only a few eighteenth-century authors who can lay claim to the title of precursor of criminology; prior to these there are, with the exception of Thomas More, hardly any who can be said to belong to this category.

6. ANTIQUITY

Most sciences have their beginning in antiquity. This, however, can hardly be said of criminology. All we can find is a few loose remarks about the subject here and there. Van Kan, in his book *Les causes économiques de la criminalité* (1903),[2] reports the results of his investigations in this field; Havelock Ellis, in *The criminal* (1889),[3] Marro in his *I caratteri dei delinquenti* (1887),[4] and G. Antonini in his *I precursori di Lombroso* (1909),[5] have done the same for the anthropological causes of crime, but the crop was a poor one.

[1] This survey does not claim to be complete. Those who take an interest in the subject I may refer to the previously-mentioned work by Van Kan, a passage from which is quoted above, and my own work, *Criminalité et conditions économiques* (1905), (second, English, edition, 1915). These two works together are, I believe, so far as criminal sociology is concerned, fairly complete. As regards the pre-history of criminal anthropology, this is very far from complete, although it is not certain that with further research much more will be discovered.

[2] *Vide* p. 15 et seq.
[3] *Vide* p. 29 et seq of the German edition, under the title *Verbrechen und Verbrecher* (1895).
[4] *Vide* p. 7 et seq.   [5] *Vide* Chapter II, p. 29 et seq.

ANTIQUITY

A few quotations from the two most important Greek authors may suffice—the Romans are without any importance whatever. Thus, Plato (427-347) says in his *Republic*: 'Man's gold has always been the cause of many crimes' (III *in fine*); 'the higher the esteem in which wealth is held, the deeper man's respect for virtue sinks' (VIII); 'It should be clear that in any State where you see poor people there must also be hidden scoundrels, pickpockets, blasphemers, and villains of every description' (VIII). Various other passages might be quoted, especially those in which he pictures the moral advantages of communism. In this Plato is the first of a long series of utopists, who were later to do the same for their own social phantasies, as we find them described in their various works. *The Laws* also contain several similar passages, such as, for instance: 'When, in any society, there is neither poverty nor great wealth, there probably prevails the highest possible standard of morality, for there will be no presumption and no injustice; nor any acts of jealousy or hatred' (III, 2).

In Aristotle (384-322) we also find a passage here and there referring to the relation between crime and society. 'Poverty engenders rebellion and crime' (*Politics*, II, 6, 13). 'The greatest crimes are not committed in order to acquire the necessary, but the superfluous' (ibid, II, 7, 13).

In addition we may mention that both these authors have also their importance for the theory of criminal law; especially Plato. It is the practical aspect of punishment which he emphasizes most strongly, and the adage: 'we do not punish because some one has offended, but in order that no one may offend', originated with him.[1]

7. THE MIDDLE AGES

In his previously-mentioned work, Van Kan publishes a very thorough and competent study of this period.[2] The

---

[1] *Vide*, concerning these authors: A. Corre, *Platon Criminaliste* (*Archives d'anthropologie criminelle XXIII*, 1908), and C. G. Gardikas, *Sur la philosophie pénale de Platon et d'Aristote* (*Schweizerische Zeitschrift für Strafrecht XXXII*, 1919).   [2] *Vide* p. 27 et seq.

28 THE PRE-HISTORY OF CRIMINOLOGY

Patristics are quite unimportant in regard to this matter and hardly worth mentioning.

Neither did the Scholastics give very much attention to the problem. St. Thomas Aquinas (1226–74) has a few passages regarding the influence of poverty on crime. 'The rich,' he writes, 'who only live for their own pleasure and waste their competence, will, when once they get down to poverty, easily come to theft' (*De regimine principum*, II, 4). 'Poverty is usually an occasion for theft' (*Summa contra Gentiles*).

Further, his lengthy defence of his thesis that, in the greatest need, theft is permissible (*Summa theologica*),[1] is of some importance.

8. THE BEGINNING OF MODERN HISTORY (SIXTEENTH CENTURY)

The first author in the history of the world who, as far as I am aware, viewed criminality in its social connexion, traced its causes to society itself, and must accordingly be ranked with the pre-criminologists in the narrower sense, is the English humanistic jurist and Chancellor under Henry VIII, Thomas More (1478–1535), author of the celebrated novel *Utopia* (1516). In this socialistic phantasy, strongly influenced by Plato, but rising far above him, a State is described, where communal ownership of the means of production exists. 'The inhabitants of Utopia,' says More, 'surpass all nations of the earth in humanity, morality, (and) virtue. . . .' The reason for this is attributed, as was done also by the numerous followers of More, to the influence of social conditions, which were so completely different in this State.

The most important section of *Utopia* for our purpose is the first book, in which More describes the conditions under which England was living in his day; he was also one of the first sociographers and social critics. The conversation gets on to the countless crimes committed in those days, and the severity of the law; thus, in twenty-four years, no fewer than

[1] *Vide* Dr. F. Schreyvogl, *Ausgewählte Schriften zur Staats- und Wirtschaftslehre des Thomas von Aquino* (1923), p. 136 et seq. from which the other quotations are also taken.

THE BEGINNING OF MODERN HISTORY 29

72,000 thieves were hanged, and this in a country of three to four million inhabitants![1] Notwithstanding this severity the flood of crime continues ceaselessly. More is not surprised at this, for with heavy punishments alone one could never stem this tide. For that one should study the causes of criminality and remove them. See to it that people are able to earn their livelihood, and crime will cease.

More then considers at length the reasons why people are unable to provide for their needs. He points among other things, to the continual wars which have been waged, one result of which was that large numbers of maimed ex-soldiers were tramping about the country. The chief cause, however, was the shocking condition of agriculture.

Since the export of wool to Flanders had become so profitable to landowners they had converted large areas of arable land into sheep pasture ('In England the sheep eat the people'), and taken away the communal pasture-land from the farmers, owing to which thousands of them were roaming about the country without any means of subsistence and so fell victims to the temptation of crime. In contrast with the abject misery of the masses we see the demoralizing luxury of the rich. But riches were easily lost; and many of those who had been spoiled by luxury might also easily become criminals when reduced to poverty. Further, numberless poor children grew up in this wicked environment and became criminals in that way.

We may finally mention that More also criticized the criminal law system of his time. Punishments, according to him, were far too heavy; as, for example, the death penalty for theft. If such heavy punishments are put on relatively slight offences, the chance of more serious offences being committed is increased, as the criminal does not thereby run any greater risk; a thought which was later also propounded by Hume. More was then already a protagonist of measures to

---

[1] By way of comparison: in the Netherlands of modern times, with a population of over eight millions only eight life-sentences were passed between 1918 and 1929!

30 THE PRE-HISTORY OF CRIMINOLOGY

force the criminal to make compensation, by working, for the damage done by him.

There is not very much more to be said about the sixteenth century, nor about the seventeenth. Van Kan quotes one or two pronouncements by Erasmus, Luther, and Calvin,[1] which, however, do not amount to anything more than remarks by the way—such as, for instance, that poverty may lead to crime. They do not testify to any insight in the social aspect of the problem.

According to Antonini, a few traces of *criminal anthropology* can be found in the sixteenth and seventeenth centuries, i.e. in the sense that some authors—he mentions G. Grataroli, *De praedictione morum naturarumque hominum cum ex inspectione partium corporis, tum aliis modis* (1554), and G. B. Della Porta, *Fisiognomica* (1586)—seek a connexion between anthropological facts and character.[2]

9. THE EIGHTEENTH CENTURY UNTIL THE FRENCH REVOLUTION

(i) *The opposition to the existing criminal law and criminal jurisprudence.* Criminal law in the latter part of the Middle Ages, the sixteenth, seventeenth, and the greater part of the eighteenth centuries was exclusively intended to serve as a deterrent and attempted to achieve this purpose by means of the most cruel punishments. The death penalty, in its most barbaric variations (generally preceded by some sharp form of torture, e.g. the rack!) and corporal punishments were quite usual forms; the idea of general prevention of crime being the chief consideration. The person of the criminal was not recognized; he was an object serving as a 'terrible example' to others, and the purely objective element of social danger inherent in the offence was the final consideration. Penal

[1] o.c., p. 38 et seq.
[2] o.c. Chapter III, p. 57 et seq. *Vide* also Marro, o.c. p. 10 et seq. In his *Symbolik der menschlichen Gestalt* (1853), C. G. Carus gives a survey of the history of the science which treats of the connexion between outward appearance and inner qualities in man (p. 40 et seq.).

THE EIGHTEENTH CENTURY 31

laws were vague (analogy in criminal law), and their formulation ambiguous.[1] The procedure in criminal cases bore a similar character. It was inquisitorial, and the accused was looked upon as a mere object of investigation; it was conducted in secret and chiefly according to documentary evidence. The law of evidence was highly arbitrary, and confession was considered to be the best form of proof; hence the torture-bench.

The grand opposition movement of the third estate against the *Ancien Régime* also drew criminal law and criminal jurisprudence into its scope. The *Aufklärung* began to shine in this field too. The Rights of Man were, henceforth, also to apply to the criminal.[2] Montesquieu (1689–1755) opened the attack, with his *Esprit des Lois* (1748), in which he entered the field against the arbitrariness and severity of the punishments, and their undue frequency.[3] The voice of humanity was heard for the first time. Rousseau (1712–78) also joined in the opposition to the cruel treatment meted out to the criminal. Voltaire (1694–1778) enters the lists in 1762, on behalf of the innocently condemned and executed Jean Calas, and becomes one of the doughtiest fighters against the arbitrariness of criminal jurisprudence of his day.[4] In 1777 a competition was held by the *Oekonomische Gesellschaft* at Bern, for a plan of a better criminal legislature. One of the competitors was J. P. Marat (1744–93), with his *Plan de législation criminelle* (1780),[5]

[1] *Vide*, amongst other works, C. G. Wichmann, *Beschouwingen over de historische grondslagen der tegenwoordige vorming van het strafbegrip* (1912), (*Reflections on the historic foundations of the present reformist movement in the conception of punishment*), Chapter II, particularly p. 60 et seq.
[2] *Vide* A. von Overbeck, *Das Strafrecht der französischen Encyclopaedie* (1902), L. Guenther, *Die Strafrechtsreform im Aufklärungszeitalter* (*Archiv für Kriminalanthropologie und Kriminalistik, XXVIII*, 1907), with extensive bibliography; also H. Schneickert, *Die Strafrechtsreformer aus dem Zeitalter der Tortur* (ibid. *XXVII*, 1907).
[3] *Vide* V. Fuchs, *Die strafrechtlichen Anschauungen Montesquieus und Friedrich des Grossen* (1924); also C. Stooss, *Montesquieus Kriminalpolitik* (*Schweizerische Zeitschrift für Strafrecht, XXXII*, (1919).
[4] *Vide* G. Masmonteil, *La législation criminelle dans l'oeuvre de Voltaire* (1901).
[5] *Vide*, concerning this author, L. Guenther, *Jean Paul Marat, der 'Ami du peuple' als Criminalist* (*Der Gerichtssaal*, Vol. 61, 1902).

while the work of J. P. Brissot de Warville (1754–93), *Théorie des lois criminelles*, had also been originally intended for this.

The principal personality in this movement was C. Beccaria (1738–94), who, in his world-famous book *Dei delitti e dei pene* (1764) gave an exposition of all the objections against the existing criminal laws and punishments; while G. Filangieri (1752–88), author of *Scienza della legislazione* (1780–5), was one of his best-known allies.

Besides the above-named authors we may mention, for England (Germany is, during this period, of little importance for our study), the jurist-philosopher Jeremy Bentham (1748–1832), founder of utilitarianism ('the greatest happiness for the greatest number'). His chief work is *Introduction to the Principles of Morals and Legislation* (1780). In 1791 he published a plan for a new kind of prison, under the title of *Panopticon, or the Inspection House*.[1] Bentham, amongst others, was one of the first protagonists of correctional punishment (*Zweck-Strafe*).

Already before the French Revolution the work of these authors had not been entirely without some results. In 1780 torture was abolished in France. In this, Frederick the Great had already preceded France in the year 1740[2]; Joseph II abolished the death penalty, and other facts of this kind might be mentioned. The greatest changes, however, originated in the French revolution.

Although the death penalty and corporal punishment were the rule, prisons had been erected here and there, from about the middle of the sixteenth century (e.g. in Amsterdam towards the close of that century). For prisoners on remand these had, of course, always been necessary.[3] Conditions in those prisons

[1] The author expresses his approval of the publication, by his friend E. Dumont, of the *Oeuvres de J. Bentham*—both a re-edition and a translation. This is probably the best edition of the works of Bentham.
[2] *Vide*, concerning this, the previously quoted book by V. Fuchs, and, further, F. Willenbuecher, *Die strafrechts-philosophischen Anschauungen Friedrich des Grossen* (1904). Frederick the Great also introduced important improvements in penal jurisdiction.
[3] *Vide*, concerning this, among others P. Pollitz, *Strafe und Verbrechen* (1910).

THE EIGHTEENTH CENTURY 33

were usually shockingly bad, both from hygienic and moral standpoints. We owe an enormous debt of gratitude to John Howard (1726–90), for having drawn attention to this state of things, in his work *The state of the Prisons* (1777); chiefly relating to England, but, in later editions, dealing also with other countries. In the seventeen-eighties a number of prison societies were founded in the United States, under pressure from the Quakers, with a view to putting an end to the highly detrimental effects of detention in association. Punishment in cells—which was to provide the proper atmosphere for introspection—was to take its place. In 1786 capital punishment was abolished in Pennsylvania.

(ii) *The Social Causes of Crime.* The *Aufklärung* literature attached great importance to the person's education; and it might therefore be expected at first sight that some attention would have been paid to this part of criminology. Such, however, was only the case to a very limited extent. One or two competitions were held, prizes being awarded for the best answers, e.g. at Groningen (1777), to which we shall return later. Some remarks on the social causes of crime are to be found here and there; but there is no evidence of any systematic treatment.

For such systematic treatment general sociology was not yet sufficiently developed, and the most important aid to criminal sociology—criminal statistics—was still lacking.

Here and there, in the writings of the Encyclopaedists and the leaders of the French Revolution, we find the connexion between crime and social environment mentioned. Montesquieu says that a good legislator will strive after prevention of crime rather than after its punishment (*Esprit des Lois*, Book VI, Chapter XI); Voltaire observes in his *Prix de la Justice et de l'humanité* (1777) that theft, etc., is the crime of the poor; Rousseau writes in the *Encyclopédie* (X, p. 575) that 'misery is the mother of the great crimes', in *Le Contrat Social* (1762) that in a well-ordered state there are few criminals, and in his *Discours sur l'origine et les fondements de l'inégalité parmi les hommes* (1753) that the institution of private ownership of the soil has brought a good many crimes in its trail. Beccaria says that theft is usually the crime of misery and despair (*Dei delitti e dei pene*, par. XXX). D'Holbach (1723–89), in his *Système Social* (1773), points out that in a society where the poor are often driven to despair crime becomes a means of subsistence. Marat, in his previously mentioned work, says that crime should be prevented rather than punished,[1] and Brissot de Warville, the man who first flung the phrase 'la propriété, c'est le vol' into the world, says, in his *Théorie des lois criminelles* that man is not born an enemy to society, but becomes one through circumstances (destitution, misfortune). The rarity of crime is in direct proportion to the efficiency of State administration.[2]

Among the so-called *utopist socialists* of this period we come across many pronouncements in which private property and crime are said to be related, as, for instance, Jean Meslier (1664–1729), in his well-known testament[3] and Morelli in the *Code de la Nature* (1753). S. N. H. Linguet (1736–94), in his *Théorie des lois civiles*, which was directed against Montesquieu, pleads that the great mass of the people has come under the yoke of private property, and that the penal code arrives on the scene when some of them actively resent this state of affairs. G. B. de Mably (1709–85) endeavours to prove that inequality of social conditions is the cause of the vitiation of 'man's natural emotions', which awakens the passions, sets people against each other, and is the cause of untold conflict (*De la législation ou Principes des Lois*, 1777). In the works of *English* socialist authors of this period one also finds passages pointing out the connexion between society and crime. Thus, R. Wallace (1697–1771), one of the precursors of Malthus in his *Dissertation on the numbers of mankind in ancient and modern times* (1753), gives in his *Various prospects of mankind, nature and Providence*, a description of a society where communal ownership of the means of production

[1] p. 29, 1790 edition. [2] p. 37.
[3] *Vide*, concerning this author and those now following, Quack, *De Socialisten*, I, Chapter X.

THE EIGHTEENTH CENTURY

exists, as a result of which theft or robbery is no longer possible.

In Jeremy Bentham's writings we also find a fairly deep insight into the social causes of criminality. He, too, wants to see crime prevented rather than punished, and enumerates a number of measures (Ferri has, later, called them *substitutifs pénaux*), which may serve this end. Thus, for instance, alcoholism, which he regards as one of the chief causes of criminality, must be combated with various means—the popularization of sport, music, the theatre, etc.[1] As an aid in the fight against economic criminality he urges the necessity of caring for those who have no longer any means of subsistence. Otherwise they just have to become criminals, and no threat of punishment can detain them.[2]

In *Germany*, an extensive range of literature was published during this time, dealing with a special type of offence, i.e. infanticide, in which certain social causes of this crime were indicated. In 1780 a competition was held at Mannheim for the best means of preventing this crime. As a result more than 400 replies were sent in![3] The best-known book on this subject, which was originally also intended for the aforementioned competition, is that by H. Pestalozzi (1746–1827), *Ueber Gesetzgebung und Kindermord* (1783), in which the author draws attention to certain social factors, such as the general moral standards of a people.

The achievements of *the Netherlands* during this period, in the field of criminal etiology, were but very modest, much the same as those in other fields.[4] Mention may be made of one of the answers to a competition held by the Groningen Society, 'Floreant liberales artes,' in 1777, entitled *Verhandeling over*

[1] *Traités de législation civile et pénale* (*Principes du code pénal*), IVme Partie, Ch. LV (*Oeuvres*, edition 1829, I, p. 193 et seq.).
[2] o.c., p. 199.
[3] *Vide*, concerning this, Dr. J. M. Rameckers, *Der Kindermord in der Literatur der Sturm-und-Drang-Periode* (1927), which work also treats of the place which crime, in that period, occupied in literature.
[4] *Vide*, concerning this, J. A. Van Hamel, *Strafrechtspolitiek van voor honderd jaar* (*De Gids*, 1909, II).

het voorkomen en straffen der misdaden, 1778 ('Treatise on the prevention and punishment of crimes'), from the pen of the lawyer H. Calkoen (1742-1818). The author looks upon poverty and unemployment as important causes of economic criminality—as a proof of which he cites the great criminality among the High-German Jews at Amsterdam.[1] Neglect of children, too, is an important factor in etiology—hence the necessity, as a preventive measure, of caring for orphans and deserted children, and the importance of good education. For the prevention of aggressive criminality he urges the necessity of spreading culture and sport among the people.

(iii) *The anthropological causes of crime.* Among the precursors of medico-anthropological theories concerning crime we must reckon the French medical man, J. O. De la Mettrie (1709-50), a pupil of Boerhaave, and author of *Traité de l'âme* (1745) and *l'Homme machine* (1748). He treats the problems in purely deterministic terms, which of course does not lead him to the conclusion that the criminal should be allowed to go scot free. 'We must kill mad dogs and crush snakes,' he says—not very soft-heartedly. La Mettrie should also be reckoned among the precursors of Gall in the sense that he shares the latter's opinion that the psychic functions are located in the brain; and he points in this connexion to the influence of toxic matter on the brain, etc., and as a result thereof, on the psyche. He is one of the first to draw attention to the significance, for etiology, of certain diseases and abnormal conditions, as for instance, pregnancy, which may set up a strong inclination to theft. He cites the case of a pregnant woman who was burnt at the stake for theft, and comments thereon as follows: 'I realize what the interests of society demand. But it is doubtless desirable that for judges only good doctors be employed. They alone could distinguish innocent from guilty.'[2] He sums up his views concerning the criminal as follows: 'The materialist will pity the vicious

---

[1] This may be of interest to those who think that the present low criminality among Jews has its origin in racial factors.
[2] *L'homme machine* (1764 edition), p. 57.

without hating them; in his eyes they will only be misshapen men.¹

The Swiss theologian, J. K. Lavater (1741–1801), author of, among other works, *Physiognomische Fragmente zur Beförderung der Menschenkenntnis und Menschenliebe* (1775–78), has also a place on the family tree of criminal anthropology; that is to say, he belongs to the precursors of the science which attempts to trace the external features (physiognomy, handwriting, gait, etc.), of character, of the emotions, etc. In his works he also deals with criminals, but his observations respecting them are not of any great importance.²

10. FROM THE FRENCH REVOLUTION UNTIL THE NINETEEN-THIRTIES

(i) *Changes in criminal law, criminal procedure, and punishments.* In 1791, the French revolution, with its Code Pénal, put an end to the criminal law and the criminal procedure of the *Ancien Régime*. A measure of uniformity, system, and precision of formulation was introduced into the new jurisprudence (no more 'analogy'); all persons became equal before the law, and with this the rights of man were recognized in this field also. Confiscation of property and corporal punishment were abolished; capital punishment was confined to a considerably smaller number of offences, and performed without previous torture; while detentionary punishments were introduced more frequently than had hitherto been the case. The lack of moderation in punishment which had prevailed during the preceding period was checked, and there was an attempt to fix the punishment proportionally to the crime. The proportion itself remained, of course, an insoluble problem; but still, the practical result was that punishment was not nearly so frequent, nor so severe as formerly. The

¹ o.c., p. 107. *Vide*, concerning this author. H. von Hentig, *La Mettrie als Kriminalanthropologe* (*Archiv für Kriminalanthropologie und Kriminalistik*, LI, 1913).
² *Vide*, concerning Lavater, amongst others, Marro, o.c., p. 14 et seq.

38 THE PRE-HISTORY OF CRIMINOLOGY

greatest improvements effected were those in criminal procedure. Proceedings were held in public during the final stages, when they took on a direct and accusatorial character. The arbitrary power of the judge was put an end to, and the law of evidence was better regulated.

After having been started in France, these reforms were also propagated and carried through elsewhere; first of all in those countries which came under French influence or rule. Thus, for example, the 'Criminal Code of law for the Kingdom of the Netherlands' was introduced there in 1809, to be replaced shortly after, when Holland was incorporated into France, by the Code Pénal. England went its own way; but there, too, under the influence of Bentham and Samuel Romilly (1757–1818), author of *Observations on the Criminal Law of England* (1810), important changes were introduced.

Conditions in English prisons (but elsewhere, too) were bad, and generally remained so, during this period.[1] Howard had, already long before this, been raising his voice in protest against this state of things, and others now came to his support—as, for instance, Bentham, Romilly, and Elisabeth Fry (1780–1845). An extensive literature began to appear; official investigations took place, and even laws were passed, which, however, were rarely put into execution. Only in the United States important changes were effected. As early as 1791 a prison consisting of cells was erected near Philadelphia by the Quakers, in which the demoralizing influence of detention in association was put an end to; but where the utter misery of loneliness took its place, the prisoner not being even allowed to work! In 1823 the so-called 'Auburn' system was introduced in New York, under which prisoners worked, in company, during the day—without being allowed to talk—and passed the night in their cells.

[1] In the Netherlands prison conditions were re-organized as far as the material side was concerned, in 1821. *Vide* about the Netherlands, e.g. J. M. van Bemmelen, *Van zedelijke verbetering tot reclasseering. Geschiedenis van het Nederlandsch Genootschap tot zedelijke verbetering der gevangenen*, 1823-1923 (1923). ('From moral improvement to the care after discharge. History of the Netherlands Society for the moral improvement of prisoners.')

The improvements which the French Revolution has effected in criminal law and procedure should not be under-rated. On the other hand, too much should not be thought of their importance either. The 'injustice' of the preceding period had been abolished; lip-service was paid to a certain 'abstract' humanitarianism; but of any actual humaneness there was, as yet, but little evidence. Punishments still remained extremely severe and hard, and the human factor in the criminal was quite ignored. Once his guilt was established he became a 'case', to be treated, as all other 'cases', to a certain—generally very large—quantity of punishment.

Improvements, were, indeed, usually of a juridical or formal character, while little or no modification was made in the actual content of the sentences. Next to sheer ignorance, the whole of the new social system must be blamed for this. In the new social order all men were equal, but only formally: their material differences were greater than ever before. True, the Code Civil does not speak of 'rich and poor', but this does not alter the fact of their existence, nor that this fact constitutes the most fundamental contrast in society. And it is just as great a fiction to put down as equals all criminals who commit the same sort of offence. They are not equals; the motives which lead them to commit a given crime are not the same, and they should not, therefore, be treated in the same way.

Punishments were mollified somewhat in the Code Pénal of 1791. This, however, was not to be for long. The French Revolution got into the hands of the extremists, 'the men with the hot heads and the cold hearts'; and these men inaugurated a most bloodthirsty and arbitrary criminal law policy, which, indeed, vied with that of the *Ancien Régime*.[1] Then, again, the period of reaction which followed (as usual), led to a renewed sharpening of punishments.[2] The Code Pénal of

[1] At the present time we are witnessing an analogous case in Soviet Russia. There, lip-service is paid to an ultra-modern criminal law policy (prisoners even get holidays!) the facts, however, point to a very frequent application of the death penalty, as well as severe terms of imprisonment (even in cases of culpable neglect, etc).
[2] A tendency to heavy punishment is usually based on three

1810 was a step backwards as compared with that of 1791. Branding was re-introduced, as well as, in some cases, torture prior to the execution of the death penalty.

In England we see the same picture. A theft of 5s. was punished in those days with death, and the same applied to more than 160 other offences!

After 1830—the great political events of 1830, and especially 1848, did not fail to exercise their influence in this respect— another new leaf was turned over; punishments became less severe and prison conditions improved. Corporal punishments disappeared almost entirely (to be reintroduced, it is true, here and there, as in Denmark in 1905, under the immortal Minister of Justice, Alberti, who afterwards turned out to be a great criminal himself!);[1] torture prior to the execution of the death penalty was definitely abolished (this form of sharpening the penalty had already been deleted, in France from the Code Pénal, in 1832); the death penalty itself was either completely abolished, as in some of the smaller countries, or restricted to a single one of the most serious crimes (murder).[2] Prisons were improved everywhere as regards hygiene, feeding, and treatment. Imprisonment in cells was introduced, following the example of America, in nearly all countries (in England in 1842), although in very different forms. In the middle of the nineteenth century England decided to adopt special legal treatment for youthful criminals, and the 'progressive' system was introduced, the most essential part of which was conditional discharge ('on parole') after expiration of three-quarters of the sentence.

However important all this may be, it has no essential factors—either combined or independent: (i) grave criminality, (ii) ideas and practice of violence in society generally, and (iii) the domination of reactionary forces, which, however lacking in insight, always have the instinct to realize that to trace the special causes of crime is for them a dangerous thing—and therefore prefer to resort to severer punishments.

[1] They were abolished again in 1911.
[2] *Vide*, concerning this, e.g. E. Roy Calvert, *Capital punishment in the twentieth century* (1927).

FROM THE FRENCH REVOLUTION 41

significance, with the exception of the last-named modifications in England. The so-called 'classical school' continued to hold sway, and judges did not concern themselves in any way with the person of the criminal. There still remained very little variety in the punishments at the judge's disposal. As Ferri said, his position was, indeed, in the majority of cases, very much like that of a doctor who has only one medicine and can only vary the dose!

From the eighteen-seventies onwards, however, another time commences, also in regard to essential principles. A great reform movement, driven on by new and mighty social forces, is started in many fields, including criminal law policy. The science of criminology rapidly develops, and leads the way, supported by a powerful drive from men out of the penitentiary camp, who were keenly dissatisfied with the results of the existing system, as shown by the high recidivism percentages.[1] A new and better period has commenced at last. Or rather, was to commence; because a considerable time elapsed ere the new light was able to shine everywhere. Holland for example, had to go through the tragedy of introducing, in 1886, a new penal code, the juridical qualities of which were beyond praise, and whose most important characteristic, the 'general minimum' (minimum of one day's imprisonment even in cases of murder) was quite in accordance with modern ideas, but which was in other respects already antiquated from a criminological point of view. And the simplicity of its criminal law system was praised as one of the chief virtues of the country! Since the beginning of the twentieth century, however, this has also changed for the better; and at the present time, thanks to its *Kinderwetten* (child laws) and the various penal law modifications introduced therein from time to time this country has won for itself a worthy place among the nations. The truth is on its way, in this field, too, and nothing can stop it!

[1] *Vide*, concerning the history of this period, E. Ruggles-Brise, *Prison Reform at home and abroad: A short history of the international movement since the London Congress, 1872* (1924).

42   THE PRE-HISTORY OF CRIMINOLOGY

(ii) *The social causes of crime.* The French Empire did not look with favour upon the study of the social sciences. Napoleon had a great contempt for 'les idéologues,' as he called them; and the same must be said of the Restoration period. The same also applies to England; although the flood of crime which the rising wave of industrialism poured out over the country[1] ought surely to have been sufficient reason for trying to find out what were its causes; however, salvation was sought rather in more severe punishment. Germany does not, for the purpose of this study, show any results at all.

In periods such as these one is obliged—this is often the case—to look for information in the opposition to the reigning powers of the day. In *England*, especially, some result may be obtained along these lines.

William Godwin (1756–1836), the first theoretical anarchist, in his *Inquiry concerning Political Justice* (1793), makes some observations on the relation between a social order, in which one man lives in plenty and the other in the deepest misery— and the existence of crime.[2] The English doctor of medicine, Charles Hall (1739–1819), in his book *The effects of Civilization on the People in European States* (1805)—an impressively worded criticism of the conditions in which the working population lived as a result of industrialism—makes the following statement on the subject: 'Civilization has a twofold effect on the morals of the people. First, by depriving them of their original share of things and reducing them to a state of both comparative and absolute poverty, it subjects them to more and stronger temptations. Secondly, by their extreme ignorance, and little sense of religion in consequence of it, they are deprived of the strongest motives to resist them. Thus, all their temptations rendered stronger, their power of

[1] F. Engels (1820–95) reports in his *Die Lage der arbeitenden Klasse in England* (1845) that between 1805 and 1830 the number of arrests for serious crimes rose from 4,605 to 18,107, i.e. by 13,502, or nearly 300 per cent, against an increase in the population of about 50 per cent! (*Vide* p. 133, 1892 edition).

[2] *Vide*, concerning Godwin: Quack, *De Socialisten*, Part I, Chapter XIV; about Owen and the French authors to be mentioned later: Parts II and III.

FROM THE FRENCH REVOLUTION 43

resistance weakened, they could not be expected to be different from what we find them.'[1]

Next to Godwin and Hall, we may mention the anarchist Th. Hodgskin (1787–1869), author of *Labour defended* (1825), and W. Thompson (about 1785–1833), author of *Inquiry into the principles of the distribution of wealth, most conducive to human happiness* (1824), but, above all, Robert Owen (1771–1858). In his work *A New View of Society, or: Essays on the formation of human character* (1816), repeated later in different other works, of which *The Book of the New Moral World* (1844) is the best known, he expounded at length his theory of this problem, which amounts to this: 'An unfavourable environment depraves a man's character, a favourable one ennobles it.' The social order of his day caused man to be bad. The masses of the people lived in the most utterly miserable conditions; they were poor, ignorant, and worked to death, children were either neglected or sent to a factory at an early age; the married woman's labour tore the family asunder; hours of labour were immoderately long; the houses in which people lived were thoroughly bad, and alcohol was their only diversion. In circumstances such as these, man was bound to become selfish. Therefore: change society, and its members will change too. If everybody is properly brought up, and has enough to live on, the standard of morals will be raised, and punishment will no longer be necessary. '. . . we hesitate not to devote years and expend millions in the *detection* and *punishment* of crimes, and in the attainment of objects whose ultimate results are, in comparison with it, insignificancy itself; and yet we have not moved one step on the true path *to prevent* crimes and to diminish the innumerable evils with which mankind are now afflicted.'[2]

Owen, who had started as a poor boy, and subsequently became a rich textile manufacturer, was a man of action. He

[1] p. 27 8. *Vide*, concerning this author, and also concerning Hodgskin and Thompson: Quack, *De Socialisten*; Supplement Volume, *A group of forgotten personalities from England of the last century*.
[2] *A New View of Society*, p. 22.

founded a model factory at New Lanark, where comparatively excellent labour conditions prevailed, such as shorter hours of labour, decent dwellings, etc. The result was, that while the flood of crime kept on rising over the rest of England, not a single criminal case occurred in New Lanark for 19 years!

In *France*, one also finds, during this period, among the so-called 'Utopist Socialists', occasional pronouncements with reference to the relation between crime and society. Thus, for instance, in Charles Fourier (1772–1837), in his *Théorie des quatre mouvements et des destinées générales* (1808), and in the Saint-Simonist Enfantin (1796–1864), in his *Enseignements* (1831–2). These, however (as in most of their closely-related English authors) are expressions of their intuition rather than of any scientific insight; proofs of their theses not usually being forthcoming. Such proofs were not to be given until a subsequent period.

(iii) *The anthropological causes of crime.* Down to the second half of the eighteenth century the insane were—just like criminals—treated as if they were in possession of a free will of their own. It was thought that they might very well have acted differently. Inasmuch as they were recognized as such they were locked up in cages, chained down, thrashed, exhibited, and if they committed a crime they were punished just as severely as the real criminals. Countless mentally-diseased persons have thus died on the scaffold! ·Under the influence of the humanitarian tendencies of the eighteenth century, but especially thanks to the discovery of the science of psychiatrics, this state of things improved. It is to the everlasting credit of the French doctor of medicine, Ph. Pinel (1745–1826), author of *Traité médico-philosophique sur l'aliénation mentale* (1791), to have been the founder of this new branch of medical science. Thanks to his activities the lot of the insane was bettered,[1] and the famous 'article 64'

[1] These improvements were not very rapid at first; in the middle of the nineteenth century, for instance, conditions in the Netherlands were still very bad (*Vide*, e.g. *Rapport der Commissie van Onderzoek inzake de verpleging en verzorging van Zenuwzieken, krankzinnigen en*

was incorporated into the Code Pénal: *Il n'y a ni crime, ni délit, lorsque le prévenu était en démence au moment de l'action*.
This non-accountability was at first limited to the few forms of insanity then known; but extended, as the science of psychiatrics progressed, to other forms (at the present time there is also partial non-accountability, i.e. in the case of what is called the 'psychopathic cases'). Next to Pinel, his pupil, J. E. D. Esquirol (1772–1840), author of *l'Aliénation mentale* (1832) and *Des maladies mentales* (1838) must be mentioned, as having also worked in this field, and performed some excellent and meritorious work. He originated the theory of the monomania's (partial disturbances in the mental powers)—which, although set aside later by more modern alienists, yet has done much to further the development of psychiatrics.

Since the close of the eighteenth century it is, therefore, no longer a matter of doubt that certain crimes have their cause in their committors' psychic deviations from the normal.

Among the precursors of criminal anthropology we must also reckon the students of phrenology F. G. Gall,[1] (1758–1828), joint author with Spuerzheim, of *Anatomie et physiologie du système nerveux en général et du cerveau en particulier* (1810–1820), and G. Spuerzheim (1776–1832), author of *Phrenology in connection with the study of physiognomy* (1826). According to this theory, each function has its organic seat in the brain; this being the precursor of the so-called 'localization theory', which, later, was to be established by P. Broca (1824–1880). According to phrenology the external signs of these mental functions were observable on the skull;

maatschappelijk ongeschikten van wege de gemeente Amsterdam (1930) (*Report of the Commission of Inquiry into the nursing and care of nerve patients, insane, and socially-unfit persons*, by order of the municipality of Amsterdam), pp. 6–7).

[1] *Vide*, concerning this author, among other things, the interesting traveller's tale, recounted by Dr. S. van Mesdag, of some Dutch students, who had followed his lectures in Paris: *Een criminologische bijdrage van het jaar 1819* (*A criminological contribution from the year 1819*) (*Tijdschrift voor Strafrecht*. XXXVII, 1927, p. 193, et seq.), also Marro, o.c., p. 17, et seq.

as, for instance, in criminology, the 'bump' of theft, that of alcoholism, etc. Subsequent criticism completely demolished these notions. In the first place, it was successfully contended that a tendency to stealing or abuse of alcohol is not a function;[1] and secondly, that the external abnormalities which were sometimes observed, were merely co-incidental. Indirectly, however, this theory did have some influence on criminology; i.e. it gave a hint of the possibility that in the brain of the criminal there exist deviations from that of other people. To the solution of this problem itself, however, phrenology has contributed nothing whatever.[2]

[1] Napoleon said about phrenology: 'Et voyez l'imbécillité de Gall: il attribue à certaines bosses des penchants et des crimes qui ne sont pas dans la nature, qui ne viennent que de la société et de la convention des hommes: que devient la bosse du vol s'il n'y a point de propriétés? La bosse de l'ivrognerie, s'il n'existait point de liqueurs fermentées? Celle de l'ambition, s'il n'existait point de société?' (*Maximes de Napoléon*, publiées par le Docteur K. J. Frederiks, II, p. 39–40). Napoleon, however, exaggerates strongly when he says: 'La nature ne se trahit pas par ses formes extérieures' (ibid, p. 40). It is not very likely that he himself ever selected anybody for a responsible post without having seen him!

[2] Among the precursors of criminal anthropology we must also class the famous French doctor of medicine, P. J. G. Cabanis (1757–1808), author of *Rapports du physique et du moral de l'homme* (1802). He has, however, made hardly any direct statements on the subject of crime. (*Vide*, concerning him, R. Maunier in the *Encyclopaedia of the Social Sciences*, III, p. 131).

CHAPTER III

THE STATISTICIAN-SOCIOLOGISTS

11. INTRODUCTORY

CRIMINAL sociology arose in the eighteen-thirties. It owed its origin to the revival of the social sciences in that period, on the one hand, and to the introduction of criminal statistics, on the other.

The social sciences had made considerable progress in France and England during the eighteenth century: Montesquieu, Turgot, Voltaire, Condorcet, Hume, Smith, and Ferguson were its most prominent representatives. As weapons in the great struggle of the third estate against the *Ancien Régime*, the social sciences had rendered excellent service. Their development was, however, to be seriously disturbed; the synthesis of these sciences, sociology *in optima forma*, was still lacking.

The French Revolution, and the twenty years' war period which was closely bound up with it; the period of reaction under Napoleon, and still more, that of the *Restauration*; all-powerful liberalism, in its second and purely individualistic phase (as an 'opposition' science it had been given a sociological bias under Adam Smith and his adherents)—all these were causes that the social sciences began to stagnate and even retire to the background. In the midst of the opposing forces, however, awakened by the *Restauration*, the social sciences once more begin to regain their place—thanks, chiefly, to the activities of Saint-Simon. The resistance to the plutocratic bourgeois monarchy, the ever-accelerating economic development, and the rapid development of the natural sciences (theory of evolution) with their inductive methods, finally caused the birth of the science of sociology *in optima forma* (Auguste Comte, 1798–1857).

Statistics, i.e. mass-observation of facts expressed in figures, also did much to further the development of the social sciences. As early as the seventeenth century, J. Grant (1620–74), author of *Natural and political observations upon the bills of mortality* (1662) discovered, while tabulating the various relevant figures, that births and deaths recurred with great regularity from year to year. The economist Sir W. Petty (1623–85), author of *Political Arithmetic*[1] (1682); the astronomist E. Halley (1656–1742), in his *An estimate of the degrees of mortality of mankind* (1693) and the theologist J. P. Süssmilch (1707–67), in his book *Die göttliche Ordnung in den Veränderungen des menschlichen Geschlechts aus der Geburt, dem Tode und der Fortpflanzung desselben erwiesen* (1741) continued these demographic and statistical studies. Petty had already, in the above-mentioned work, commenced the study of economic statistics; C. King (1648–1712), Charles Davenant (1654–1714), A. Young (1742–1820), followed.

In this way an important beginning had been made with the practice of statistics—but no more than that. In the first place, statistics lacked a theoretical foundation, and students of them were mostly empiricists pure and simple. In the second place, the material with which one was obliged to work was still far from reliable, and rested on estimates, rather than on properly counted figures—the State having, in those days, little or no concern for such matters. In both these respects, however, far-reaching changes were eventually to make their appearance.

In France, the great mathematicians M. J. A. de Condorcet (1743–94), in his *Tableau général de la science qui a pour objet*

[1] The history of the word 'statistics' is a remarkable one. They were originally called 'political arithmetic', which name was later altered by the French statisticians into 'social arithmetic'. In the seventeenth and eighteenth centuries the meaning, in Germany, of the word *Statistik* (derived from statista, i.e. statesman) was the peculiar features of a state, description of a people, and suchlike. The students of this branch of knowledge hardly ever employed figures, and had a deep revulsion against 'political arithmetic'! The change of name occurred later, and the word 'statistics' took the place of 'political arithmetic'. In England Y. Sinclair (1754–1835) used the word 'statistics' for the first time. (*Vide* V. John, *Geschichte der Statistik*, I, 1884.)

INTRODUCTORY 49

l'application du calcul aux sciences politiques et morales (1795), P. S. de Laplace (1749–1827), in his *Théorie analytique sur les probabilités* (1812), and J. Fourier (1768–1829), provided statistical science with the theoretical foundation of which it stood in such great need, by relating it to the mathematics of probability. It was finally the Belgian mathematician and sociologist Ad. Quetelet (1796–1874), who definitely founded statistics as a scientific method; and he was also the founder of practical statistics in Belgium, as well as the organizer of the international statistical congresses.

The modern, centralized state, which began to take form at the end of the eighteenth and the beginning of the nineteenth century, felt an ever-growing need of statistics. Napoleon's dictum: 'La statistique, c'est le budget des choses et sans budget point de salut publique' leaves no doubt upon this point. The civil status registers were introduced by him, which in turn formed a basis for the population registers— the latter becoming eventually one of the most important sources of factual information for demography. The United States held the first census of the population in 1790, followed in 1801 by England and France; trade statistics improved; in short, the steady improvement of the statistical groundmaterial dates from this time. Not only was the material further improved upon, it was also extended into other departments of social life, as in France, with the introduction of criminal statistics (*Compte Général de l'administration de la justice criminelle en France*), whereby, for the first time, a scientific study of criminality (and later also of other sociopathological phenomena, e.g. suicide) was rendered possible; whereas, in former times, intuition and deduction had prevailed in this field. What we call 'moral statistics' were, in fact, born.

12. CRIMINAL STATISTICS AS A STATIC METHOD

A few years after the introduction of criminal statistics in France, some authors made a beginning with the collecting

50 THE STATISTICIAN-SOCIOLOGISTS

and elaborating of the figure-material relative to the subject. One of the first of these was the Frenchman A. M. Guerry (1802–66), the originator of the name *statistique morale*. In his *Essai sur la statistique morale de la France* (1833) we find some data concerning sex and age in relation to criminality. The geography of crime in France (*statica*) is also dealt with in this work. From the maps contained in the book it is evident that in the richest provinces (i.e. in *total* wealth) the greatest number of offences against property took place; a fact which causes Guerry to remark that a great total wealth may very well imply that it is very unequally distributed and that it must therefore be accompanied by great poverty. Apart from this Guerry has not concerned himself much with the etiology of crime; for him it is rather a means of ascertaining the moral standards of a people at any given period.

The most prominent personality in this field is the above-mentioned statistician Quetelet[1]. It is due to him that criminal statistics have become such an aid to criminal sociology. It was also due to his work that criminality was shown, for the first time, to be a social fact. In his work *Sur l'homme et le développement de ses facultés; ou Essai de physique sociale* (1835), of which the second, largely-revised edition was called *Physique sociale, ou Essai sur le développement des facultés de l'homme*, he set out at length his pioneering view on the subject.

Quetelet observed, in the first place, that crimes—murder, for example—keep recurring from year to year with punctual regularity, even down to the details and the manner of their commitment. To illustrate this, he gives a survey of the figures, derived from French statistics. As this table has a certain historical significance it is reproduced on p. 51.

Quetelet's own commentary on these figures may also be

---

[1] Quetelet was also the first criminal-statistician. As early as 1828 he drew attention to this new method, in a communication to the *Académie Royale de Bruxelles* (*vide* J. Lotin, *Quetelet, statisticien et sociologue* (1912), p. 119.

STATISTICS AS A STATIC METHOD

TABLE I

	1826	1827	1828	1829	1830	1831
Meurtres en général	241	243	227	230	205	266
Fusil et pistolet	56	64	60	61	57	88
Sabre, épée, stylet, poignard, etc.	15	7	8	7	12	30
Couteau	39	40	34	46	44	34
Bâton, canne, etc.	23	28	31	24	12	21
Pierres	20	20	21	21	11	9
Instruments tranchants, piquants et concordants	35	40	42	45	46	49
Strangulations	2	5	2	2	2	4
En précipitant et noyant	6	16	6	1	4	3
Coups de pied et de poing	28	11	21	23	17	26
Le feu	0	1	0	1	0	0
Inconnus	17	1	2	0	2	2

called historical, and it may therefore be of interest to quote the passage in full:

'In everything connected with crime the same numbers repeat themselves with a regularity there can be no mistaking, even in the case of crimes which, it would appear, must be entirely beyond all human foresight, such as murders, since these are committed in general as a result of brawls, which arise without motives, and apparently in the most fortuitous circumstances. However, experience proves that not only do murders take place annually in almost the same numbers, but the weapons which are used to commit them are employed in the same proportions. What is one to say then of crimes which are the result of forethought?

'This regularity with which the same crimes are repeated annually in the same order and are visited with the same penalties in the same proportions is one of the most curious facts taught us by the statistics of the courts. I have made a point of drawing attention to it in my various writings: I have not ceased to repeat each year: *There is a budget which is defrayed with terrifying regularity by the prisons, the bagnio's, and the scaffold, and it is one which, above all, every effort must be made to reduce:* and each year the figures appear to confirm what I foretold to such an extent that I might have said perhaps with more accuracy: a tribute which man pays with more regularity than that which he owes to nature or to the State Exchequer is that which he pays to crime. Sad condition of humanity! We can foretell in advance how many people will stain their hands with the blood of their fellows, how many will be forgers, how many will be poisoners, almost as one can foretell in advance the births and deaths which are to take place.

'Society contains in itself the germs of all future crimes. It in some degree prepares for them and the criminal is only the instrument which carries them out. Every social order therefore pre-conditions a certain number and assortment of crimes which result as a necessary consequence from its organization.'[1]

From the above words it has been concluded that Quetelet was a fatalist, and that according to him humanity had better resign itself to the fact of crime with the same equanimity as if it were a natural phenomenon not to be avoided. Nothing could, of course, be further from the truth; the very words at the end of the passage quoted above indicate that in Quetelet's opinion crime can be combated by improving the conditions under which humanity lives.

In the second part of his *Physique Sociale* the writer examines various factors which exercise an influence on 'le penchant au crime'—i.e. the greater or lesser tendency to the commitment of any given crime—such as, for instance, education, profession, poverty, climate, changes in the seasons, etc. (he had previously dealt with the increase in economic crime during

[1] *Physique sociale*, I, pp. 95-7.

STATISTICS AS A DYNAMIC METHOD 53

the winter, and crimes against persons in the summer)—and further, the influence of sex and age. His study of the two last-named factors has become a classic, not one of the moderns having had occasion to alter it to any considerable extent. Criminality among women is much less than among men; among men it increases rapidly from fourteen years of age onwards, reaching its climax at about the twenty-fifth year. In the case of women this curve runs a similar course, only a few years later. After this the curves show a gradual decline.

13. CRIMINAL STATISTICS AS A DYNAMIC METHOD

The dynamic element in criminality was not denied by Quetelet, but, on the contrary, recognized in express terms. It was only natural, however, that during his first investigations—which only occupied a few years, and during which no very important social events occurred—the static element was, primarily and chiefly, in evidence. As further data, however, covering longer periods and different countries, became available, one began to get some conception of the 'movement' of criminality, while still retaining the view that much of it was of a constant nature. The study of these movements became especially important when it was found possible to relate them to important social changes which occurred during the same periods.

The first author to establish this connexion was the Belgian statistician and criminologist Edouard Ducpétiaux (1804–68), who in his book *Le paupérisme dans les Flandres* (1850) pointed out that the violent crisis of 1845–8 (industrial crisis and failure of the potato-crop) brought in its trail a very considerable increase in crime, which actually went up from 8,984, in 1845, to 16,782 in 1847; an increase of eighty-seven per cent! 'C'est donc un fait bien constaté: l'accroissement de la criminalité dans les Flandres a marché de pair avec l'extension de la misère.'[1]

[1] o.c., p. 47.

54 THE STATISTICIAN-SOCIOLOGISTS

L. M. Moreau-Christophe (1791–1888), in his *Du problème de la misère et de la solution chez les peuples anciens et modernes* (1851), points to the connexion, in England (1814–48) between industrial development and the sharp increase in pauperism;

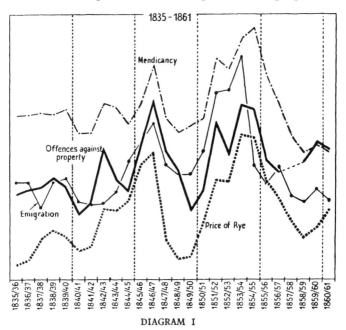

DIAGRAM I

THEFT AND GRAIN-PRICES IN BAVARIA, 1835–61

According to G. von Mayr *Statistik der gerichtlichen Polizei im Königreiche Bayern und in einigen andern Laandern*.
(Reprinted from E. Roesner. *Der Einfluss von Wirtschaftslage, Alkohol und Jahreszeit auf die Kriminalität* (1930)

one of the results of the latter being, again, a rise in criminality.

The strictly-religious A. von Oettingen (1827–1905) shows, in his work *Die Moral-Statistik in ihrer Bedeutung für eine Sozialethik* (1868), that in times of crisis, theft, etc., especially by women and children, increases; while in times of prosperity,

STATISTICS AS A DYNAMIC METHOD 55

on the other hand, it is aggressive criminality which shows a rise.

The most important author in this period is the celebrated German statistician G. von Mayr (1841–1925), who, in his *Statistik der gerichtlichen Polizei im Königreiche Bayern und in einigen andern Ländern* (1867) showed that during that period a relation of very close parallelism existed between thefts, etc., and grain prices. 'Every penny increase in the price of grain during the period from 1835 to 1861 means an increase in the number of thefts of one per 100,000 inhabitants'[1] (see Diagram I).

According to Von Mayr this increase is caused by what he calls *objektive Nahrungserschwerung*—i.e. a rise in prices, owing to which a large number of people are no longer able to provide for their primary necessities.[2]

Investigations such as those mentioned above were continued during the years following, and their results have been confirmed on all sides.[3] During the 'seventies and 'eighties, however, they were rather pushed to the background, owing to the development of another theory with which we shall deal in the next chapter.

---

[1] p. 42. The book in question is hard to obtain. Von Mayr, in his *Die Gesetzmässigkeit im Gesellschaftsleben* (1877), has reprinted the most important parts from it.

[2] We shall return to this question later, in Chapter V.

[3] In the above only a few of the most important authors are mentioned. For a more exhaustive treatment, *vide* Von Kan, o.c., Ch. VIII, p. 373 et seq., and Bonger, o.c., Ch. II, p. 36 et seq, in the American edition, p. 30 et seq.

CHAPTER IV

THE ITALIAN OR ANTHROPOLOGICAL SCHOOL

14. INTRODUCTORY

(i) THE *pre-history, between the beginning of the eighteen-thirties and 'seventies.* In the second chapter it was pointed out that the phrenologists Gall and Spuerzheim ought in a certain sense to be ranked with the precursors of criminal anthropology, although their teaching itself lacked a proper scientific foundation. Their labours were continued by the French Doctor of medicine H. Lauvergne (1797–1859), who was attached to the prison of Toulon, and the author of *Les forçats considérés sous le rapport physiologique, moral et intellectuel* (1841). Apart from certain views on phrenology (which were subsequently proved to be erroneous) the book contains some interesting psychological and sociological observations. C. G. Carus (1789–1869), in the work which I have mentioned elsewhere (*Symbolik der menschlichen Gestalt* (1853)), also discusses the relation between deviations in the formation of the skull, as observed in criminals, and backward mental propensities. L. M. Moreau-Christophe, as is evident from his book *Le monde des coquins* (1863), is still strongly under the influence of Gall, Spuerzheim, and even Lavater. Meanwhile, the entire doctrine of phrenology had succumbed under the hammerblows of criticism, and had practically disappeared from literature altogether. Towards the end of the 'fifties P. Broca (1824–80), founder of the *Société d'anthropologie de Paris* (1859) established scientific anthropology. Examinations of criminals' skulls had already been made by him; these, however, had led him to no other conclusion than that the anomalies discovered by him were sometimes of a pathological character.

We have seen that Pinel and Esquirol had shown lunacy, in some cases, to be a cause of crime. It was on these lines

INTRODUCTORY 57

that anthropological investigation proceeded during this period; and indeed, it may be asserted without fear of justifiable contradiction that medical science in those days inclined very strongly towards looking upon the criminal as a pathological case. The line of thought which runs through Esquirol's doctrine has a parallel in the labours of the English anthropologist and alienist, J. C. Prichard (1786–1848), author of *Treatise on insanity and other disorders affecting the mind* (1835). What is called 'moral insanity' (i.e. moral colour-blindness, without other mental disturbances) was first diagnosed by him.

P. Lucas (1805–85), in his *Traité philosophique et physiologique de l'hérédité naturelle*, I (1847), argues that a criminal tendency is fundamentally present at birth, and is hereditary; circumstances playing a merely occasional, though not unimportant part.

About the middle of the century, A. B. Morel (1809–73), in his *Traité des dégénérescences physiques, intellectuelles et morales de l'espèce humaine et des causes qui produisent ces variétés maladives* (1857), published his celebrated doctrine of degeneracy, according to which the normal human being may degenerate, in his descendants, in the course of a few generations, as a result of unfavourable circumstances. This degeneration may also lead to crime.

E. Dally (1833–87), in his brilliant attack on the doctrine of the free will, *Considérations sur les criminels au point de vue de la responsabilité* (1863), points out the relation which exists in some cases between insanity and crime: 'Crime and insanity are two forms of organic cerebro-mental decay.'[1]

H. Maudsley (1835–1918), in his work *Physiology and pathology of mind* (1867), and especially in his *Crime and insanity* (1872), defends the thesis that a certain proportion of criminals are a degenerate variety of the human species. Thus, he says:

'Between crime and insanity there lies a neutral zone; on

[1] *Annales médico-psychologiques*, XXI, 1863, p. 260 et seq.

one side only a little madness and much perversity, on the opposite edge perversity is less and madness is supreme.'[1]

Other English alienists of this time, J. B. Thompson (1810–73), in 'On the hereditary nature of crime' (*Journal of Mental Science*, 1870), and in 'Psychology of criminals' (1870 or 1875); D. Nicolson (1845–1932), in 'The morbid psychology of criminals' (*Journal of Mental Science*, 1873–5); and the Italian G. Virgilio (1836–1907), in his *Sulla natura morbosa del delitto* (1874) take up a somewhat similar standpoint.[2]

We must further reckon among the precursors of the anthropological school the founders of the theory of evolution —not in the restricted sense of the term, since they did not pronounce upon the problem of criminality; but in a more general sense; they laid the foundation upon which it became possible for criminal anthropology to arise. These were: J. Lamarck (1744–1829), in his *Philosophie zoologique* (1809), E. Geoffroy Saint Hilaire (1772–1844), in *Sur le principe de l'unité de composition organique* (1828), and chiefly, Charles Darwin (1809–82), in his '*On the Origin of Species by means of natural selection*' (1859), and '*The Descent of Man*' (1871). Neither should, of course, Herbert Spencer (1820–1904), whose *First Principles* appeared in 1862, be forgotten in this connexion.

(ii) *The personalities and their work.* The most prominent personality of the Italian school is C. Lombroso (1835–1909), a medical man, first a professor of juridical medicine, later also professor of psychiatrics at Turin. His principal work is *L'Uomo Delinquente* (1876), followed later by *Pensiero e*

[1] p. 32 of *Le crime et la folie* (1888), the French translation of the last-named book.
[2] The above *exposé* makes no claim to completeness. *Vide* also Marro, o.c., p. 21 et seq., Ellis, o.c., p. 35 et seq., and X. Francotte, *L'anthropologie criminelle* (1891), p. 9 et seq. P. Despine, whom several authors mention in this connexion, was no criminal-anthropologist, but the first scientific criminal-psychologist. We shall return to him later. In the literature on the subject, J. L. Casper (1796–1864) is also sometimes mentioned as being a precursor of Lombroso —quite wrongly, however. (*Vide* his *Mörderphysiognomiën, Vierteljahrschrift für gerichtliche und öffentliche Medizin*, VI, 1854).

INTRODUCTORY 59

Meteore (1878), *Il delitto politico e le rivoluzioni* (1890), in collaboration with R. Laschi (1861–1905), *La donna delinquente, la prostituta, e la donna normale* (1893), in collaboration with G. Ferrero (1871); *Gli anarchici* (1894), and also *Le crime, causes et remèdes* (1899). Lombroso has also written on the origin of genius *Genio e follia* (1864), and on the subject of pellagra, which at that time was of frequent occurrence in Italy.[1]

In *Italy* itself, Lombroso has had a large number of adherents and fellow students of criminal anthropology.[2] The most important are: E. Ferri (1856–1929), professor of criminal law at Rome; author of (amongst other works) *I nuovi orizzonti del diritto e della procedura penale* (1881), *La sociologia criminale* (1884); further, the jurist R. Garofalo (1852), *La criminologia* (1884); the alienist A. Marro (1841–1913): *I caratteri dei delinquenti* (1887); S. Sighele (1868), *La folla delinquenta* (1892).

In other countries the Italian school has not found anything like the same adherence. In *France* and *Belgium* not a single one of the better-known criminologists can be classed in the anthropological ranks; in *England*, up to a point, Havelock Ellis (1859), author of *The Criminal* (1889); in *Germany*, only H. Kurella (1858–1916), in his *Naturgeschichte des Verbrechers* (1893), and R. Sommer (1864), in his *Kriminal-Psychologie* (1904); while the Swiss E. Bleluer (1857), in his book *Der geborene Verbrecher* (1896), must also be ranked with the anthropologists. In *Germany*, Lombroso's theories have lately been finding more adherence again, as is evident from the establishment of the *Kriminalbiologische Gesellschaft*. Its leader there is the Austrian, A. Lenz, author of *Grundriss der Kriminalbiologie* (1927). In the *Netherlands* the only writers who can be regarded as adherents (and even this only with a certain reserve), are C. Winkler (1855), in his *Iets over*

[1] *Vide* the biography by Dr. H. Kurella, *Cesare Lombroso als Mensch und Forscher* (1910).
[2] The reason why criminal anthropology happened to originate in Italy is probably partly accidental. Crime, however, is very widespread in that country, which naturally forced the problem to the fore.

60   THE ITALIAN SCHOOL

crimineele anthropologie, 1895 (*On criminal anthropology*), and the first free-lance professor of criminal anthropology in the Netherlands, Dr. A. Aletrino (1858–1916), author of *Twee opstellen over crimineele anthropologie* (1895) (*Two essays on criminal anthropology*), and of one of the few existing text-books on the subject, *Handleiding bij de studie der crimineele anthropologie* (1904) (*Manual for use in the study of criminal anthropology*).

In other European countries, too, the Italian school is said to have made a few adherents here and there.[1] I am not in a position to give any information concerning these, as I have not mastered the languages: I am, however, under the impression that the authors in question are of no great importance. In the *United States* a live interest in the subject only began to be taken during the last twenty years; i.e. since the establishment, in 1909, of the 'American Institute of Criminal Law and Criminology'. The anthropological theory found a fairly considerable measure of adherence there during the first years of the existence of this Institute; but this interest waned later on. The chief author there on this subject is W. Healy (1869), in his work *The Individual Delinquent* (1915).[2]

15. THE THEORY OF LOMBROSO

(i) *Introductory*. In *L'uomo delinquente*,[3] no definition of crime precedes the actual treatment of the problem. Winkler once said, in the pointed way peculiar to him: 'Only jurists ask for definitions. Everybody else knows that a definition can only be properly given at the end of an investigation—and,

---

[1] *Vide*, concerning this, L. von Thót, 'Die positive Strafrechtsschule in einigen Europäischen Ländern' (*Monatschrift für Kriminalpsychologie und Strafrechtsreform*, VIII, 1911, p. 401). About the Spanish-speaking countries *vide* C. Bernaldo de Quiros (1873), *Modern theories of criminality* (1911), p. 100 et seq.
[2] *Vide*, concerning the United States, the article *sub voce* 'Criminality', by H. E. Barnes, in *The Encyclopaedia of the Social Sciences*, IV, in which the most important literature is mentioned.
[3] I have used the German translation by M. O. Fraenkel, *Der Verbrecher* (1894).

THE THEORY OF LOMBROSO 61

even then, only perhaps—because it will of necessity be incorrect, even then. For, as a matter of fact, the science on which the definition is based, is never complete.'

If 'definition' is taken in the sense of 'all-comprehensive conclusion', then Winkler's remark is, of course, quite correct. One may, however, also take 'definition' as meaning a more or less provisional defining or limiting, with no other purpose than to avoid misunderstanding. Times out of number discussions have been completely abortive, because the opponents were not even talking about the same subject! We shall see that the lack of a proper definition, as referred to above, has actually been the cause of frequent misunderstandings.

The argument starts—along the lines of the theory of evolution in its early beginnings—with a dissertation upon crime . . . *amongst plants*! Flesh-eating plants are classed as criminals![1] This—need it be said—has, of course, nothing to do with crime; first result of the lack of a definition. Throughout nature different species of living beings fight each other; the one serves the other as food, and there is no sense at all in stamping this as crime.

After this introduction the *animal kingdom* appears on the criminological stage. Actions of one species of animal towards the other—also towards man—are cited; even to the classic example of the cat stealing the fish!

Coming to animals of the same species—it is, of course, only among these that crime could ever be thought of— Lombroso mentions the fight for the female (sexual selection), and for the position of leader of the herd. But surely, to qualify all these acts as having even the remotest connexion with crime, one must, so to speak, wear a permanent pair of criminological spectacles in one's views of nature! Lombroso, of course, acknowledges this, up to a point; and mentions, as genuine equivalents of crime, those instances in which

[1] Manouvrier justly ridiculed this idea, in his *La genèse normale du crime* (*Bulletin de la Société d'anthropologie de Paris*, 1893). He reproaches Lombroso not to have gone far enough: he should have involved chemistry into the question as well, which teaches us that one kind of matter may also destroy the other.

animals living in herds (horses, cattle, elephants, etc.), occasionally expel troublesome specimens of their kind. Admittedly, one might, with a large dose of goodwill, agree that here is something remotely comparable with a case of pathological criminality.

The way is now clear for *primitive humanity* to be drawn into the scope of the argument. Now, according to Lombroso, aboriginal man must be looked upon as a born criminal: '. . . (among savages) crime is not considered an exception, but practically as the general rule; in fact, nobody looks upon it as such; on the contrary, its first appearances are, rather, ranked in the same class with the most irreproachable actions.'[1] Lombroso then proceeds with an attempt to prove this thesis. Without the slightest notion of ethnology, with an utter lack of critical sense, and often from the worst possible sources of information, a few facts are dragged in to prove that primitive man was a born criminal (thief, raper, murderer), and primitive woman a prostitute!

This bold contention is wholly and absolutely untrue. In the first place, Lombroso evidently still takes up the standpoint of natural law. He is a complete stranger to the notion that moral conceptions are never fixed, but change according to time and place. To take only one instance: infanticide occurs fairly frequently among the most primitive peoples (nomads); and is not considered by them as immoral. This is to be explained by the difficult circumstances under which they live, and which may force them to adopt this course of action. If they acted differently the whole group to which they belong might perish. There is no question of any inborn hard-heartedness at all, or even of a lack of love for the children. Steinmetz proved that primitive peoples have great devotion and parental tenderness for any of their children which they are in a position to rear.[2] An analogous case is the killing of the aged (or their suicide) among nomadic peoples.

[1] o.c., p. 35.
[2] *Das Verhältniss zwischen Eltern und Kindern bei den Naturvölkern* (*Zeitschrift für Sozialwissenschaft*, I, 1898).

THE THEORY OF LOMBROSO 63

Both these moral conceptions and practices disappear completely as soon as these nomads become settlers, and take to agriculture, whereby they are enabled to rear more children and maintain their aged.

In the second place, Lombroso makes no distinction between actions within, and outside, the group (this phenomenon was called by the Russian sociologist Kulischer 'ethical dualism').[1] Various facts mentioned by him relate to other groups than the one to which he who committed the act belonged, and therefore rank with acts of war, and not with crimes at all. Within the group itself crime is a rare exception, and mutual care and devotion attain a very high standard. The available material evidence of this is simply overwhelming; and I may confine myself to quoting one or two summary judgments: '. . . the normal savage exists only as a devoted member of the group whose customs he respects and whose every interest he defends; the savage is a great lover of children,' says Steinmetz in his *L'ethnologie et l'anthropologie criminelle*.'[2] Hobhouse sums up his opinion in the following words: 'The typical primitive community . . . is a little island of friends amid a sea of strangers and enemies.'[3]

As a matter of fact, in modern sociology the hypothesis that primitive man was fundamentally a-moral and only grew into a moral being as time went on, must be considered a fatuity. The known facts of ethnology and history, as well as of psychology, are too flagrantly in contradiction with such ideas.

Hardly less erroneous are Lombroso's pronouncements on 'the criminal in the child'; they are also quite in keeping with the same line of thought. Here, he presents us with the

[1] In our modern, greatly complicated form of society, man is a member of different groups at one and the same time, which is the cause of continual and serious inner moral conflicts. One should therefore speak to-day of 'the pluralism of ethics'.
[2] *Compte Rendu des travaux de la cinquième session du Congrès International d'anthropologie criminelle à Amsterdam, 1901*, p. 100–1.
[3] *Morals in Evolution* (1908), I, p. 280. For more extensive information concerning this, *vide* my own *Criminalité et conditions économiques*, p. 438 et seq. (American edition, p. 383 et seq.); also *Over de evolutie der moraliteit* (*On the evolution of morality*) (1922), p. 7 et seq.

following amiable picture of the human child: '. . . that the germs of moral abnormality and criminal nature do not occur as exceptions, but as the rule, in the first years of human life; exactly in the same way that we find, regularly, certain forms in the embryo which—if they occurred in grown-ups—would rank as abnormalities; so that the child would appear to be a human being lacking in moral sense—what alienists call *morally defective*; but what we prefer to call a *born criminal*.'[1] He then cites a number of instances of children's mendacity, cruelty, jealousy, etc.

Now, modern child psychology has made hay of this representation of the child as being either a little devil or an angel.

'Ni cette indignité, ni cet excès d'honneur'. There is no point whatever in attributing to children an inborn knowledge of the content of moral dicta; but this failing has no more sinister meaning in regard to their morality than lack of knowledge has in regard to their intellectual endowments. Besides, children are impulsive—functioning primarily—owing to lack of experience of life, which is just as little proof of their moral inferiority; and as every one knows they are often just as impulsive in acting altruistically. Cruelty in children is, more often than not, entirely unconscious; they inflict pain, for instance on animals, without knowing it, and they change their conduct as soon as they understand what is actually happening. True, children are very often untruthful in their statements; but this, too, is in the majority of cases quite unconscious and has its origin in their uncontrolled imagination. And when they do tell real lies this cannot possibly be of anything like the same gravity as in the case of adults; they just cannot realize its seriousness and implications. There are, of course, children—but they are very rare—who resemble the picture drawn by Lombroso; but in these cases one has to do with moral idiots or imbeciles, and not with children of sound mental propensities.[2]

[1] o.c., p. 97.
[2] About this matter, *vide*, e.g. A. Fischer, *Psychologie der Gesellschaft* (*Handbuch der vergleichenden Psychologie*, II, 4, Ch. VIII, p. 434 et seq.).

THE THEORY OF LOMBROSO 65

(ii) *The anthropology of the criminal.* Taking the views outlined above as his starting-point, Lombroso then proceeded to examine anthropologically a large number of criminals in various prisons—more especially their skulls. The conclusion which he drew from these examinations was that, in the criminal, peculiar anthropological features are in evidence. Thus, for example, the capacity of the skull (especially in the case of thieves) is held by Lombroso to be smaller than that of normal persons, while, in addition to this, there are supposed to be several other anomalies about the criminal's skull. In the brain, too, Lombroso notices deviations from the normal, which remind him of animal formations—although he was unable to point to any specific 'criminal' deviations. Further, their physiognomy was also supposed to differ from the normal: large jaws, crooked faces, receding foreheads (*front fuyant*), etc., he found to be of frequent occurrence. Finally, low sensibility, and tattooing—as among primitive peoples— were frequently found to exist.

The conclusion to which Lombroso came was that in the majority of cases the criminal is an entirely separate species of human (*genus homo delinquens*)—such as, for instance, the negroes. He is born like that (*il delinquente nato*). He is not predisposed, but predestined to crime, and no change of environment can make any change in this respect whatsoever. This innate tendency, moreover, may be recognized in outward peculiarities, so that there exists, according to Lombroso, a criminal type, which we are actually able to diagnose. 'Crime, therefore, would appear to us to be a *natural phenomenon*'[1]—these are the final words of his *L'uomo delinquente.*

(iii) *The atavistic hypothesis.* The question now arises: how can the origin of this kind of abnormal being be accounted for? In his attempt to solve this problem Lombroso hit on the following quite ingenious hypothesis. Granted that primitive man was a-moral, and only acquired his moral qualities in the course of time, then the criminal must be an atavistic phenomenon, a throw-back; i.e. he suddenly shows again

[1] o.c., p. 537.

those peculiarities which his immediate ancestors had lost, but which his remote ascendants had possessed. We may call this 'throw-back heredity'.

This hypothesis, however, was just as erroneous as it was ingenious. In the first place—as we have already seen—its starting-point is untenable from an ethnological-sociological view-point—which rather makes the whole hypothesis fall to the ground. In the second place, it was attacked from medico-anthropological quarters; and shown—apart from the numerous errors and inexactitudes which are usual features in Lombroso's investigations—to rest upon an entirely wrong interpretation of the facts.

M. Manouvrier, anthropologist at Paris University, whom we have already had occasion to refer to, makes the following observations concerning Lombroso's theory:

'Among these anatomical characteristics found among detained criminals there are several which have nothing abnormal or even harmful in them; there is none which can serve to characterize a criminal; there is none to which one could attribute this imaginary physiological property which constitutes an impulse to criminal acts, not even the famous *fossette vermienne* of the occipital which, according to the rather malicious remark of Professor Benedikt, might at most indicate a disposition to haemorrhoids.

'None of these characteristics by itself could be accused of constituting an innate disposition to crime. Is, then, the combination of several of them any more dangerous? Not at all. There is no man in whom one cannot find some muscular anomaly or other which recalls a conformation proper to apes or quadrupeds.

'Perhaps one will say that if anatomical characteristics appearing to indicate a partial throw-back are not dangerous by themselves they constitute at least a kind of symbol, a sign of anatomical and psychological atavism too generalized for us to be able to define it with our present methods of investigation, and that they must be the sign of a tendency

THE THEORY OF LOMBROSO 67

to act like savages, pre-historic men, pre-human ancestors. That is a speculation for which there is no scientific justification. On the contrary, we know that these anatomical characteristics, abnormal in our species and considered as reappearances of ancestral characteristics, can exist without the individuals possessing them being irregularly disposed in other ways or having any special instincts. They are simply morphological accidents, purely local and compatible with the most favourable disposition.'[1]

Jelgersma, in his study *The Born Criminal*, also criticizes Lombroso's hypothesis on the origin of crime. After admitting that certain observations would seem to confirm the existence of this kind of atavism, he continues:

'In general, however, Lombroso's opinions appear to me to be quite erroneous. The atavistic theory does not apply to the majority of degenerative features, such as unequal eyes or ears or, indeed, all a-symmetry; abnormal hair-growth, crooked skulls, etc.; none of these deviations can be said to exist also among savage tribes or closely-related species of animals.

'Neither does the theory apply to functional degeneration. A narrowing of the eyesight, such as Ottolenghi frequently observed among criminals, or abnormalities in any of the other sense-organs are none of them properties which we can properly describe as atavistic; on the contrary, they remind us strongly of pathological modifications.

'On the other hand, the view that degenerate features are correlative changes is a much more feasible one. In regard to this it is, of course, not at all impossible that those correlative changes may occasionally be of an atavistic nature. On the contrary, this would seem quite conceivable, if one bears in mind that, as a result of this unknown sequence of

[1] *La genèse normale du crime*, pp. 415–7. *Vide* also, by the same author, his attack on Lombroso, at the Criminal-anthropological Congresses at Paris (1889) and Brussels (1892) (*Actes du IIième Congrès International d'anthropologie criminelle, Actes du IIIe Congrès*, etc.).

causes and effects, which separates the primary from the correlative modification, the organism re-acts in such a way as to cause either an arrested development or a faulty one. Only in those cases where such an arrested development occurs in a certain organ or faculty, would one be justified in speaking of "atavism", for only then is it to be expected that forms of organs which were peculiar to our ancestors should be met with once more. If, on the other hand, the organism re-acts by developing in a faulty way, then one may confidently say that there is nothing in the form or the function of the organ which was also peculiar to our ancestors—and that is usually what happens. In both cases, the conception of the degenerate feature as a correlative modification, in the sense explained above, may be thought perfectly feasible.'[1]

It would be an easy matter to multiply the number of authorities who have pronounced themselves hostile to the atavistic hypothesis. As a matter of fact it has now been completely abandoned. In its place, the pathological hypothesis, which had previously occupied such an important position, has returned, also among Italian criminologists.

(iv) *The pathological hypothesis.* For some time, Lombroso and his adherents held the view that the criminal was an epileptic. This, however, they were unable to maintain. It is not even certain that the percentage of sufferers from epilepsy is greater among criminals than among other people.

After this, there came a return—to some extent—to the theory of Morel: the criminal is a degenerate. His anatomical deviations were held to be signs of degeneracy.

The first question which then arises, is: is it really a fact that all or the great majority of criminals are degenerates? This question must be answered with an emphatic negative. Lombroso gives high percentages of signs of degeneracy among criminals. His critics, however (besides Manouvrier we ought to mention the German criminologists Baer and

[1] *Tijdschrift voor Strafrecht*, VI, 1892, pp. 106–7.

THE THEORY OF LOMBROSO 69

Naecke), have commented very unfavourably on these figures —and Lombroso was, as is generally agreed, not a very careful investigator. In the second place, these figures by themselves do not prove anything much. They have, of course, to be compared with the corresponding figures among non-criminals. When this is done it becomes evident—as is also clear from the passage, quoted earlier, by Manouvrier—that countless non-criminals show similar anthropological deviations. Naecke found among the nursing staff of a large institution a mere three per cent who did not show some sign or other of degeneracy! And on the other hand, countless criminals, some of them the most serious cases, have absolutely nothing anthropologically abnormal about them![1] If all criminals were degenerates, and all non-criminals normal, there would, indeed, be strong evidence of a close connexion between the two phenomena; but there is absolutely no question of that.

We may therefore assume that the only justifiable conclusion is that there is a larger percentage of degenerates among criminals than among non-criminals. In other words, a degenerate is sooner pre-disposed to crime than a non-degenerate. This is, of course, nothing to be surprised about; degenerates sooner become losers in the struggle for existence, and therefore sooner tend to lapse into crime. The majority of criminals hails from the lower strata of the people—this is a fact proved by criminal-sociological data—where degeneracy is more frequent than elsewhere. Baer ends his masterly work:

'Crime ... is not the result of any special organic condition of the criminal; an organic condition peculiar to the criminal and which forces him to commit criminal acts. The habitual, apparently "born" criminal possesses many outward signs of physical and mental deformity, but these are neither collectively nor singly of such well-marked peculiarity as to distinguish and characterize him as something typical

[1] Professor Spielmeyer reports, in the *Archiv für Kriminologie* (B. 90, p. 252), that the mass-murderer Kuerten had perfectly normal brains, and did not show any anatomical deviations which pointed to any psychic disorder, either acquired or innate.

among his fellows and contemporaries. The criminal carries with him those traces of degeneration which occur frequently among the lower strata of the population from which he generally originates; which (traces), having been acquired or inherited in certain social conditions of life, assert themselves, in him, with intensified violence.'[1]

Apart from the above, it should be recognized, in regard to a certain (taken altogether, only a small) proportion of criminals, that their psychic abnormalities are the direct cause of their a-social conduct. But to stamp them, for no better reason than that, as 'born criminals', is simply to violate the facts.[2] In this category also, social environment still plays some part—generally an important one.[3] Those cases where the psychic abnormality is so great that the individual in question is driven to committing crimes *in any circumstances* (moral imbeciles, etc.), belong to the rare exceptions. Usually they are very soon recognized as such, and placed into some institution suitable to their case.

(v) *The criminal type*. What has been said above already renders it highly improbable that the outward features mentioned by Lombroso as having been observed in criminals, are of such a kind as to justify our speaking of a 'criminal type'. I may perhaps be allowed to make one more remark in this connexion.

During the 'nineties criminal anthropology aroused considerable interest in the Netherlands, and was fairly widely studied there. Several medical men, among whom were Winkler, Berends, and Aletrino, took skull measurements of criminals and other categories of persons. In Aletrino's *Manual for use in the study of Criminal Anthropology* (I, p. 171)

---

[1] p. 411.
[2] Compare in this connexion the very pointed remarks on 'the born criminal'—who probably never commits a crime—by J. V. van Dÿck, *Bijdragen tot de psychologie van den misdadiger* (1906) (*Contributions to the psychology of the criminal*), p. 1 et seq.
[3] Also indirectly, through vitiation of the foetus (as in the case of alcoholism). This subject will not be dealt with in this book.

THE THEORY OF LOMBROSO 71

we find the results of these examinations tabulated (see p. 73) (Table II).

From the figures printed in italics Berends has drawn the following conclusion: '. . . murderers, paroniacs, epileptics, and imbeciles are buds on the same stem, and this stem is a lesser development of the cerebral skull, and a greater development of the facial skull.'[1]

To me, a layman in anthropology, it would seem that a good many facts of quite different, but nevertheless remarkable nature may be deduced from this table—although the expert can, no doubt, get much more out of it still. In the first place, it strikes me that in the majority of the measures taken no pronounced differences are noticeable at all; and that, where they are, they keep within fairly narrow limits. In the second place, it is evident that the material which has been compared is not homogeneous; for that, the differences between the non-criminal groups are too great, which points to the probability of the influence of racial difference. The most important thing, however, is that, repeatedly, *the differences between the murderers and the non-criminal groups* (e.g. *their antipodes, the policemen) are considerably smaller than between two non-criminal groups, as for example, the policemen as against the soldiers*; e.g. *in the linea bigoniaca, three per cent and twelve per cent respectively!*

Winkler, expressing himself with more caution than Lombroso, and refraining altogether from speaking of a 'criminal type', says, in reference to the above figures: 'The judge unconsciously chooses subjects with narrow foreheads and large jaws.' Now what exactly are the implications of this statement? Manouvrier had pointed out, years ago already, that very powerful men usually had large jaws[2]. So the mountain has borne a mouse; and what it amounts to is this: among murderers we find a relatively large number of muscular people! One might say, indeed: to be aware of that one need not be a criminal anthropologist!

[1] Quoted according to Aletrino, I, p. 170.
[2] *Vide La genèse normale du crime*, p. 415.

The latest, and probably also the most thorough-going criticism of the anthropological doctrine was made by the English prison doctor Charles Goring (1870–1919), who, in his *The English Convict* (1913)[1] reports the results of investigations made by him into 3,000 of the gravest criminal cases. His conclusions destroy in every respect the theories of Lombroso and his adherents. The length of skull of Oxford and Cambridge students, on the one hand, as compared with that of convicts, on the other, shows no noticeable difference; while the difference in the same measurement, as between Aberdeen and Cambridge students, is greater than that between the students and the convicts! And between Professors of London University and convicts there is not even a mentionable difference in these measurements! 'In fact'—says Goring —'from the knowledge only of an undergraduate's cephalic measurements, a better opinion could be formed as to whether he was studying at an English or a Scottish university than a prediction could be made as to whether he would eventually become a University professor or a convicted felon.'[2]

What applies to skull measurements applies equally to other anthropological data. To take only one more instance: tattooing. This occurs, percentagewise, more frequently among soldiers than among criminals! It is, on the whole, not surprising that Dr. Goring's general conclusions as to the physical type of the criminal is that 'Our results nowhere confirm the evidence, nor justify the allegations of criminal anthropologists. They challenge their evidence at almost every point. In fact, both with regard to measurements and the presence of physical anomalies in criminals, our statistics present a startling conformity with similar statistics of law-abiding classes. The final conclusions we are bound to accept until further evidence, in the train of long series of statistics, may compel us to reject or to modify an apparent certainty— our inevitable conclusion must be that *there is no such thing as a physical criminal type.*'[3]

[1] In 1915 an abbreviated edition appeared under the same title used by me.   [2] o.c., p. 80.   [3] o.c., p. 97.

TABLE II

Measures	Winkler 50 doctors	Deknatel 50 soldiers	Aletrino 50 police inspectors	Aletrino 50 police sergeants	Aletrino 50 police constables	Aletrino 50 journalists	Aletrino 50 firemen	Berends 50 paranoiacs	Berends 50 epileptics	Berends 50 imbeciles	Winkler 50 murderers
Horiz. circumference	570·74	561·76	563·62	552·64	557·20	560·36	550·64	550·64	554·86	548·32	561·82
Linea b.nauricularis	128·10	127·30	139·46	135·70	135·48	135·40	134·56	129·68	128·98	127·88	128·23
Major width of forehead	141·00	139·16	144·54	142·26	138·84	141·56	140·32	134·20	136·32	133·74	135·51
Minor width of forehead	110·24	111·24	110·88	110·10	111·62	109·92	109·84	107·46	106·54	105·88	108·82
Major lin. bizygom.	140·20	138·12	142·14	138·84	139·90	135·88	140·18	140·16	139·08	138·00	140·24
Minor lin. bizygom.	117·86	109·20	104·92	108·10	107·54	105·70	104·48	122·72	120·94	119·88	114·57
Linea bigoniaca	97·48	93·48	106·68	104·42	107·00	101·78	102·54	108·58	108·14	105·96	110·31
Line from ear to chin	290·38	278·72	305·58	301·12	297·80	299·56	297·56	283·14	290·78	285·32	294·66

Major width of forehead, i.e. width as measured between the parietal bones.
Minor „ „ „ „ „ „ points next to the eyes.
Linea bigoniaca „ „ „ „ „ lower jaw angles.

Must we, therefore, conclude from our refusal to admit the existence of a 'criminal type' that there is no relation at all between the external appearance of a person and his character? Not in the least. Most people are rightly convinced that such a connexion does, in fact, exist. We all take an interest in the face of a person whose acquaintance we wish to make; some of us would notice the way he walks; others, how he shakes hands; others again would look at his hand-writing, etc., etc. Kretschmer, in his book *Körperbau und Charakter* has inaugurated the systematic study of this relation; up to now, we had relied mainly on our intuition in this matter. So far, it is only a beginning. One thing, however, is certain; this relation is not of the coarsely elementary nature which Lombroso imagined it to be, and, indeed, Kretschmer resolutely denounces the theories of Lombroso.[1] We should also bear in mind that this study is concerned with the connexion between *character* and certain outward features, and not between these features and *criminality*. There are numerous criminals of quite decent disposition, while on the other hand there are countless non-criminals with extremely bad characters. It is, surely, the height of ingenuousness to imagine that all bad people fall into the hands of the law!

(vi) *Conclusion. The influence of Lombroso on the practice of criminal law.* The net result of the Lombroso theory is, generally speaking, not a very great one. Neither his theory of the 'born criminal', nor that of the 'criminal type' has stood the test of time. It must, however, be admitted that he has succeeded in consolidating the conception, which had arisen already prior to the eighteen-seventies, that the criminal ought to be considered a pathological case, a degenerate; and it is largely to his credit that at present this side of the problem is being given so much more serious attention, *in foro*, than it used to be in former times. Nevertheless, he has very greatly over-estimated the importance of this aspect of the matter.

---

[1] '. . . der Verbrecher oder "der Entartete" ist kein biologischer Typus, weder in körperlicher noch in psychischer Hinsicht' (Chapter III, p. 44, 7th edition).

THE THEORY OF LOMBROSO

The number of degenerates, among criminals, whose crimes are to be attributed to their mental aberration is not nearly so large, by a long way, as Lombroso contended. The importance of environment, in the genesis of what we call pathological criminality has been greatly underrated by the Italian school, and this school has also paid insufficient attention to those social factors which, by way of heredity, have an influence on degeneration.

In one respect, indeed, the anthropological school has actually arrested the development of criminology to some extent; i.e. by suggesting that the criminal is an abnormal being from a biological point of view. One must have lived during that time to understand fully the power of that suggestion. This contention really amounts to an abuse of the word 'normal'. Manouvrier has formulated this as follows:

'Because certain acts are incompatible with the efficient functioning of society, and for that reason are called *abnormal* (whence comes the epithet *normal* applied on the contrary to useful acts and to their authors), there is no reason to transport this antithesis into the region of biology in opposing the word *normal* (in its physiological sense) to the word *criminal*. Nothing justifies such a comparison. Abilities physiologically quite normal can be used for acts equally normal physiologically, but which from the social point of view will be called abnormal, as being contrary to social prosperity.'[1]

Setting aside pathological criminality, the criminal is driven by motives of a perfectly similar nature to those of the non-criminal, although they may, of course, differ quantitatively. Moreover, the means he employs are, biologically speaking, just as little abnormal. Even killing another man cannot, strictly speaking, be called 'abnormal'; the mere thought of war should make that plain. The abnormal element in crime is a social, not a biological element. With

[1] o.c., pp. 451–2.

the exception of a few special cases, crime lies within the boundaries of normal psychology and physiology. Such is the basic principle of criminal sociology.

Disregarding for a moment the fact that in the history of science negative results may also have their importance, and are, in that case, just as much to the honour of him who achieved them as positive results are, we may frankly say that Lombroso's merits in the field of criminal law are exceptionally great. He has, indeed, given the impulse to a revolutionary movement the effects of which cannot, as yet, be estimated. In the beginning of the 'seventies the 'classic school' still reigned supreme. Against this school the Italians engaged in a fierce struggle, and carried it through with indomitable persistence. Not only did they win great and brilliant victories, but what is more, the result of their efforts is that practically all students of criminal law, including those who oppose them in principle, find themselves forced, willy-nilly, to follow their lead. The history of criminal law in all countries proves this in the most convincing way. It will be the everlasting merit of the Italian school to have been instrumental in ensuring that it is no longer the concept 'crime', but the person of the criminal, his propensities and environment, which are becoming more and more the centre of interest *in foro*.

16. THE THEORY OF FERRI

Out of all Lombroso's adherents it is Ferri who has done the most creditable work in spreading the doctrine. He was a brilliant orator, a smart debater, and one who plied a ready pen; and endowed with these gifts, he made the theories of Lombroso known in every quarter, attacking the classic school incessantly.

As a man of science he was the first to see that Lombroso's theory was, in its original form, untenable. Without, however, attacking its essential principle, he succeeded in re-shaping it in such a way as to make it less one-sided, by recognizing the influence of the environment-factor. In this way he prevented

THE THEORY OF FERRI

its being completely wrecked. He succeeded in getting the other representatives of the school on his side—even Lombroso himself. This is proved by the latter's book *Le crime, causes et remèdes*, published in 1898.[1] In this work the social causes of crime are dealt with, as well as the individual ones. The defeatist standpoint—that no remedy exists for crime—is here abandoned.

In his *Sociologie criminelle*, Ferri had spoken of *substitutifs pénaux* (correctional measures which may take the place of punishment). Lombroso speaks of the 'canalization of crime', and, in other places, of 'symbiosis'—which, in this connexion, means the application to a useful purpose of the criminal's bad tendencies.

In this book, Ferri gives the following formula for the origin of crime: 'Every crime is the resultant of individual, physical and social conditions'.[2] Sometimes one factor is of greater importance, and at other times another; the individual element being, however, the most important on the whole: 'Social environment gives crime its form; but its origin must be sought in biological anti-social tendencies (both organic and psychic)'.[3]

This view was shared later by several other authors; one may, indeed, safely say that it is, at present, the generally prevailing one. Its adherents form what is called the 'biosociological' school. We shall deal with this school separately, further on in this book (chapter VI).

---

[1] The publication of this book was an event of great importance for criminology. The same cannot be said of the work as such. It is superficial and confused, and evinces some very curious conceptions of causality. A single instance: Lombroso mentions some author or other, according to whom the percentage of smokers is greater among criminals than among non-criminals; and then proceeds: 'One can see clearly from this that there exists a causal relation between tobacco and crime' (p. 121)! A good Italian book on the economic causes of crime is the one by E. Fornasari di Verce (1869), *La criminalità e le vicende economiche d'Italia* (1894).
[2] French edition of 1893, p. 161.
[3] o.c., p. 43.

CHAPTER V

THE FRENCH, OR 'ENVIRONMENT' SCHOOL

17. THE FRENCH SCHOOL IN THE RESTRICTED SENSE

'Die Welt ist mehr Schuld an mir, als ich.'
H. EULENBERG

WHEN, in the eighteen-seventies, Lombroso and his school propounded the anthropological doctrine, the French medical world opposed it from the start. In so doing it remained in the tradition of J. Lamarck, E. Geoffroy St. Hilaire, and also of L. Pasteur (1822–95), all of whom had laid great stress on the tremendous importance of environment, in the formation of species and varieties, as well as for the etiology of infectious diseases. These authors did not, however, link up with the statistician-sociologists,[1] who were, essentially, also environment-theorists. Their labours consisted largely in laying the emphasis more on the environment theory, and in denouncing the theory according to which crime was an innate element in human character. They were medical men, not sociologists—although they frequently evinced a striking insight into the social causes of crime.

The *chef d'école* was the Professor of juridical medicine at the University of Lyons, A. Lacassagne (1843–1924). He had already taken a firm stand against Lombroso at the 1st International Criminal-Anthropological Congress at Rome, in 1885. After denouncing the atavistic hypothesis he formulated the environment doctrine in the following terms:

'The important thing is the social milieu. Allow me a comparison borrowed from modern theory. The social milieu is the culture-medium of criminality; the microbe is the criminal element which has no importance until the day when it finds the culture which sets it multiplying.

[1] *Vide* Chapter III, p. 47 et seq.

THE FRENCH SCHOOL 79

The criminal with his characteristics, anthropometric and otherwise, only seems to us to have a very mediocre importance. All these characteristics can be found besides in quite honest folk.'[1]

He ended his speech with the words which were one day to become famous: 'Societies have the criminals they deserve.'[2] Some other publications on the criminal problem by Lacassagne have appeared. The most important of these is *Marche de la criminalité en France*, 1825–80.[3] In 1886 he founded, together with G. Tarde, the *Archives d'anthropologie criminelle, de criminologie et de psychologie normale et pathologique*, which was for a long time the leading criminological journal; unfortunately, however, it became one of the victims of the Great War, and had to stop publication in 1914.

Another and equally important personality in this field is the anthropologist L. Manouvrier (1850–1927), professor at Paris University, whom I have already mentioned.

At the Second International Congress for Criminal Anthropology, held in Paris in 1889, it was chiefly Manouvrier who fought Lombroso on his own ground. A commission was then appointed, consisting of seven well-known anthropologists, among whom were Lacassagne, Magnan, Benedikt (Vienna), and Manouvrier, for the purpose of making a comparative study of a hundred criminals and a hundred non-criminals. This commission did not, however, perform its task. It did not even meet a single time. The reason for this was reported by Manouvrier at the Third International Congress, held at Brussels in 1892: the Italians had stayed away from this Congress out of spite and irritation. Otherwise they might have been able to attend the funeral of their own doctrine—that the criminal is a species of *homo sapiens* which can be diagnosed anthropologically.

Apart from the above-mentioned work *La genèse normale du crime*, Manouvrier has published a few other studies on the

[1] *Actes du Premier Congrès International d'Anthropologie Criminelle*, p. 166.
[2] Ibid., p. 167.
[3] *Revue scientifique*, 1881.

subject of criminology; as, for example, *Les crânes des suppliciés* (*Archives d'anthropologie criminelle*, I, 1886) and *L'atavisme et le crime* (*L'ère nouvelle*, 1894).

The third important personality of the French school is G. Tarde (1843–1904), jurist and sociologist. From the very commencement, in his book *La criminalité comparée* (1886) he was a powerful opponent of the Italian School.

According to Tarde, criminality is not an anthropological, but a social phenomenon, dominated, in exactly the same way as other social facts, by *imitation*.[1] 'Tous les actes importants de la vie sociale sont exécutés sous l'empire de l'exemple', he says in his *Philosophie pénale* (1890).[2]

Indeed, the element of imitation in society is, generally speaking, of tremendous importance. More than ninety per cent of people are completely devoid of any originality and slavishly conform, in their habits, ideas of life, religion, etc., to the environment in which they have grown up. The remaining small percentage is only slightly original in some small department of their thoughts, and is, in every other way, just as imitative. This is also evident from the steady continuity of society, and the usually slow rate at which modifications take place. In the field of criminality, too, there are undeniable truths in Tarde's theory of imitation. All novel kinds of crime are immediately copied by other criminals, while of all the many causes of criminality not one is, surely, so prominent and important as the corrupt environment from which the majority of criminals hail. But although the significance of imitation for criminal etiology is great, Tarde has not been able entirely to avoid exaggeration. To compare, as he does, present-day vagrancy with itinerant minstrels of medieval times is to make oneself ridiculous. Imitation may give an explanation of why an already existing social phenomenon extends itself, or maintains itself over a long period (tradition); but it cannot, of course, shed any light on how this phenomenon came into existence.

[1] His chief work is entitled *Les lois de l'imitation* (1890).
[2] p. 323, 4e édition, 1903.

THE SCHOOL OF ECONOMIC ENVIRONMENT 81

Other authors on the same lines are, e.g. E. Laurent (1861–1911), *Les habitués des prisons de Paris* (1890), and *Le criminel aux points de vue anthropologique, psychologique et social* (1908); J. Soquet (1853–1925), *Contribution à l'étude de la criminalité en France de 1826–1880* (1883); A. Bournet (1854–96), *De la criminalité en France et en Italie* (1884); P. Aubry (1858–99), *La contagion du meurtre* (1894); A. Corre (1841– ?), *Les criminels* (1889), *Crime et suicide* (1891), *L'ethnographie criminelle* (1894); M. Raux (1842–1915), *Nos jeunes détenus* (1890); E. Régis (1855–1918), *Les régicides dans l'histoire et dans le présent* (1890).

The German criminal anthropologist A. Baer (1834–1908), author of *Der Verbrecher in anthropologischer Beziehung* (1893), also belongs to the 'environment-school'; while to a large extent P. Naecke (1851–1913), author of *Verbrechen und Wahnsinn beim Weibe* (1894)[1] must also be ranked in the same class.

18. THE 'ECONOMIC ENVIRONMENT' SCHOOL

When speaking of the precursors of criminal sociology (Pars. 8–10), we saw that several authors, the majority of whom were socialists, attached great importance to economic conditions in the etiology of crime. This tendency was rather accentuated at the end of the eighteenth and the beginning of the nineteenth century, when a new economic system made its appearance, and a sharp rise in criminality was observed.

It was to be expected that the new theory in the sociological field, which arose about the middle of the nineteenth century, namely the economic view of society, or historic materialism, would have a great influence on criminology. According to this theory, economic factors in society are, dynamically speaking, primary, and statically speaking, fundamental. This theory found its classic formulation in Marx's *Zur*

[1] *Vide Archiv für Kriminal-Anthropologie und Kriminalistik*, XXI p. 188, in which Naecke declares himself to have become almost completely a supporter of the theory of environment.

Kritik der politischen Oekonomie (1859). 'The system of production of material life,' he said, 'conditions the social, political, and spiritual processes of life generally.'[1] Lacassagne's dictum: 'Every society has the crimes which it deserves,' should, according to the theory of Marx, be read as follows: 'every system of production (e.g. the feudal, the capitalistic, etc.) has the crimes it deserves.' Along this line of thought, therefore, the question is not only to what extent economic factors (e.g. destitution) play a part in originating crime, but to what degree any economic system dominates the whole of criminality, in the last analysis, and throughout all strata of society.

The first author who should be mentioned in this connexion is the Italian, F. Turati (1857–1932), who recently died in exile as an opponent of Fascism.[2] In his little work *Il delitto e la questione sociale* (1883) he criticizes, in the first place, the Italian School. In the more positive part of this book he argues that it is not only necessity and destitution, but also covetousness—which has a close connexion with the present economic system—that leads to economic crime. With regard to offences against persons—aggressive criminality—Turati points to the significance of the influence which material conditions have on the human mind: destitution renders it obtuse; while its companions, ignorance and coarseness, are also mighty factors in the genesis of this kind of crime. Bad housing conditions have a lowering effect on sexual morals and are the cause of moral offences.

N. Colajanni (1847–1921), in his *Sociologia criminale*, also takes a stand against the anthropological doctrine. He points to the connexion between economic crises and the increase in economic crime, between crime and other 'socio-pathological' phenomena such as prostitution—which in their turn are rooted in certain economic conditions, and to the economic sub-soil of political crime. Colajanni also emphasizes the

[1] p. XI, *Vorwort* (1897 edition).
[2] The majority of the authors now about to be mentioned are not supporters of Marxism in the narrower sense; they did, however, strongly come under its influence.

THE SCHOOL OF ECONOMIC ENVIRONMENT 83

relation between the economic system and the general component elements of criminality: private property makes man's character selfish, and thereby brings it closer to the committing of crime. The best prevention of crime is an economic system in which the maximum of stability and a minimum of lack of proportion in the distribution of wealth has been attained.

Among the authors writing in the same trend we must mention A. Bebel (1840–1913), author of *Die Frau und der Sozialismus* (1883); B. Battaglia (?–1890) *La dinamica del delitto* (1886), P. Lafargue (1842–1911) *Die Kriminalität in Frankreich, 1840–1886*,[1] published in 1890; and P. Hirsch (1868) *Verbrechen und Prostitution* (1897).

The merit of these authors is that they have focused attention in a precise manner on one definite aspect of the *Théorie du milieu*, which had remained rather vague in the hands of the French authors, who were mostly medical men. But however great the merits of their work may have been (in particular is this so with Lafargue's study) it cannot be maintained that they have succeeded in proving their thesis; they have made it acceptable, no more.

19. SOME ETIOLOGICAL RESULTS OF CRIMINAL SOCIOLOGY

Criminal sociology is already about a century old, and it can boast of having brought complete clarity into some of the factors in criminality. It is not even possible to mention all the material in this concise survey of criminology, let alone deal with it exhaustively. We must therefore confine ourselves to drawing attention to a few of the more important results obtained.

(i) *Neglect of Children, etc.* Criminality among children and young persons forms in itself a large part of total criminality. Moreover, the overwhelming majority of adult criminals began their career, or were already demoralized, while still young. One pretty well knows the causes of adult

[1] *Die Neue Zeit*, VIII.

criminality when one knows those of youthful crime. The accumulated material which proves that bad example, neglect, etc., are very important factors in causing criminality, is simply overwhelming.[1] We give some selections from this material.

FRANCE

Etablissements d'éducation correctionnelle

	Boys per cent	Girls per cent
Semi-orphans	31·7	37·1
Orphans	6·2	17·4
Parents sentenced	17·0	43·0
Parents, beggars or prostitutes	7·8	23·1
Parents unknown or run away	6·5	10·0[2]

Quartier correctionnel de Lyon

	per cent
Incited to crime by parents or by their example	8
Deserted (wholly or morally)	38
Bad training (either weak, impotent, or violent)	41
Normally brought up	13[3]

Raux—the author, from whom these last data are derived, notes in this connexion the category 'normally brought up', does not at all mean 'well brought up'—for that, too much is often lacking.

[1] Of the special literature I may mention J. M. Baernreither, *Die Ursachen, Erscheinungsformen und die Ausbreitung der Verwahrlosung von Kindern und Jugendlichen in Oesterreich* (*Schriften des Ersten Oesterreichischen Kinderschutzkongresses, 1907*, I), G. Gregor and G. Voigtländer, *Die Verwahrlosung* (1918), also Gruhle's work, which will be quoted later.
[2] Calculated according to *Statistique Pénitentiaire* (1890–5).
[3] M. Raux, *Nos jeunes détenus*, pp. 17 and 9.

SOME ETIOLOGICAL RESULTS

ENGLAND

Industrial Schools

	Boys per cent	Girls per cent
Orphans	3·4	6·7
Semi-orphans	31·3	36·2
Deserted by parents	5·7	7·8
Father and/or mother criminals, etc.	3·5	5·5
Illegitimate	6·8	32·2
Others	49·3	11·6
	100	100[1]

The last category 'Others' does not at all mean that these children grew up in a good environment. The contrary is true. One of the most expert witnesses who appeared before the Royal Commission on Reformatory and Industrial Schools, declared that this was only true in about six per cent of the cases.[2]

Dr. C. Burt produces the following data about youthful criminals in London:

	Boys per cent	Girls per cent	Together per cent
Father dead	10·6	14·9	12·2
Separated, or deserted family	6·5	13·5	9·1
Mother dead	10·6	19·0	13·7
Separated, or deserted family	5·7	8·2	6·6
Both father and mother dead or deserted family	1·6	6·8	3·5
Stepfather or stepmother	19·5	35·2	25·3
Illegitimate	6·5	9·5	7·6[3]

[1] F. Toennies, *Jugendliche Kriminalität und Verwahrlosung in Gross Britannien* (*Zeitschrift für die gesamte Strafrechtswissenschaft* XIII, p. 904).
[2] W. D. Morrison, *Juvenile Offenders* (1896), p. 148.
[3] *The Young Delinquent* (2nd edition, 1927), p. 64.

As regards the percentage of illegitimacy, Dr. Burt notes that this is, for births in London, four per cent, but that the morality among these children is three times as high as that among legitimate children. This remark is quite correct; but it should have been added that legitimizing and adoption also occur frequently.[1] The percentage of illegitimates among the adult population accordingly amounts in no case to more than one per cent. In Germany (where the general percentage is high) it is certainly not more than three per cent, from which we may conclude that criminality among illegitimates is extraordinarily high.

With regard to the moral conditions in the families of youthful delinquents, Dr. Burt reports, further, that in more than half the cases much was lacking in this respect (sexual immorality, drunkenness, fighting, etc.); while in nearly eighty per cent of the cases order and discipline in the home was insufficient (either too weak or too severe).[2]

THE NETHERLANDS

Dr. J. P. F. A. Noorduijn, who for a long time was attached as alienist to State Reformatory Schools, submits the following figures, relating to boy criminals residing at the Observation Home at Alkmaar.[3]

	per cent
Father alcoholist	26
Mother alcoholist	6
Mother prostitute or 'kept'	7

[1] *Vide*, concerning this, e.g. O. Spann, *Untersuchungen über die uneheliche Bevölkerung in Frankfurt a/M* (1912), and the *Onderzoekingen naar de levensomstandigheden der in 1911 en 1912 te Amsterdam buiten echt geboren kinderen en hunne Moeders*' (1923) ('Inquiries into the living conditions of children born out of wedlock during 1911 and 1912, and their mothers, held by the Poor Law Officers at Amsterdam').

[2] o.c., p. 65.

[3] 'De observatie, na de invoering van de Kinderwetten in het Rijksopvoedingsgesticht te Alkmaar' ('Observation, after the introduction of the Child Laws, in the State Reformatory school at Alkmaar') (*Tijdschrift voor Strafrecht*, XXIII, 1922).

SOME ETIOLOGICAL RESULTS

	per cent
Father sentenced	5
Mother sentenced	5
Parents separated	7
Father dead	17
Mother dead	14
Both dead	3

Seventy-five per cent of these cases hail from families with five or more children.

BADEN

Zwangserziehungsanstalt in Flehingen

	per cent
Father sentenced	70
Mother sentenced	42
Father and/or Mother alcoholist	34
Lost father before 15 years of age	26
Lost mother before 15 years of age	24
Lost both before 15 years of age	10[1]

SWEDEN

Dr. D. Lund reports the following facts, from an investigation made by him:

Moral condition of the parents of youthful criminals

	Per cent
Father bad character	56
Father doubtful	10
Mother bad character	49
Mother doubtful	9
Both parents bad	35
Both parents good	22

Orphans were 15 per cent, semi-orphans 47 per cent, the

[1] H. W. Gruhle, *Die Ursachen der jugendlichen Verwahrlosung und Kriminalität* (1912).

THE FRENCH SCHOOL

father was an alcoholist in 36 per cent, the mother in 6 per cent of the cases.[1]

On surveying the above material—and the total available evidence only confirms this—we clearly see the overwhelming importance of environment during youth, for the genesis of criminality. In a large number of cases conditions are so shocking that no predisposition to crime whatever need be present; these are what is called the purely environment cases.[2] We shall deal later with the factor of predisposition present in other cases; and merely point out that among youthful delinquents hardly any cases occur which hail from well-to-do and civilized surroundings—although, of course, this predisposition to crime exists there just the same.

The flood of youthful crime which had been running over various countries as they became involved in industrialism forced the authorities everywhere to take special measures, such as disciplinary education, and the like. It has been possible to arrest this flood—leaving alone special circumstances, such as the War period—and, indeed, to cause it to recede. This is surely some indication that the environment theory is right. A further confirmation of this can be found in the results of disciplinary and other special education. Nobody would expect success in all cases—for that, the evil is often too deeply-rooted; while conditions after the subject's return into society are often too utterly unfavourable. A doctor could not cure all illnesses either—especially serious and chronic ones—and when he does cure a patient he cannot guarantee that in unfavourable circumstances he will not fall ill again. This, of course, is not to say that in a large number of cases the illness might not have been prevented altogether.

[1] *Ueber die Ursachen der Jugendasozialität* (1918).
[2] At the time of writing (April-May 1932), a most interesting biography of one of the gravest criminals in the Netherlands ('Boef'), from the pen of Brusse, is appearing in the *Nieuwe Rotterdamsche Courant*, in which it is proved that among those people there are some who are not, essentially, criminal characters at all.

SOME ETIOLOGICAL RESULTS 89

In the years 1923 and 1924 an inquiry was instituted by the Central Statistical Bureau into the 'government-children'. Out of 1,363 men (minimum age 25 odd, maximum 32 years odd; i.e. from 5 to 11 years after their discharge) 52 per cent had not again been sentenced; out of 210 women (same ages), 84 per cent. Of the so-called 'guardians-children' (who do not differ very much from the 'government-children'), about 80 per cent of the men were successful, and about 95 per cent of the women.[1] Taking into account the fact that the 'government-children' are the most difficult cases from a criminal law point of view, and that the mere fact of a sentence does not prove that the case is an absolute 'failure', the above figures may be taken as evidence that the environment theory is correct. On the other hand we must not forget that the absence of a sentence is in itself no definite proof that the case is a complete 'success'.

It is for these reasons that the 'Netherlands League for the Protection of Children' held a similar inquiry, but on a different basis. The criterion which was taken for 'success' or 'failure' was not sentence or acquittal, but information obtained as to the children's conduct. A disadvantage of this method is the more or less subjective element which is thus brought into play. The result of this inquiry, which covered 2,270 cases, is as follows:

	'Guardians' children Per cent	'Government' children Per cent
Conduct good	65	61
Conduct fair	20	12
Conduct bad	7	17
Died	6	4
Abnormal	2	6
Total	100	100

[1] M. G. L. Suermondt, ('De resultaten van het Rijksopvoedingswezen') ('The results of State Reformatory Education') (*Tijdschrift voor Strafrecht*, XXXV, 1925, p. 299).

Leaving the two last-named groups ('died' and 'abnormal') out of consideration, the percentages are, for the quite successful cases, about sixty-six per cent, and inclusive of the group 'fair', about eighty per cent.

If one sub-divides the cases according to the age at which the children began their disciplinary education, the results are found to be still more striking (see table below).

The sooner the children are, therefore, taken away from their environment—or, to put it differently: the sooner they show their criminality—the better the results are: of the youngest cases only seven per cent were failures:

SUB-DIVISION ACCORDING TO THE AGE AT WHICH
CHILDREN ARE TAKEN AWAY FROM THEIR ENVIRONMENT[1]

Years of age	Good	Fair	Bad	Died	Abnormal	Total
Up to 14	67	18	7	6	2	100
14 to 16	65	17	9	5	4	100
16 to 18	64	15	12	4	5	100
18 to 21	53	14	29	1	3	100
Unknown	48	21	12	15	4	100

Neglect, desertion, etc., are among the causes of criminality of every description, and are, therefore, a general factor. We shall now deal with some other causes, which apply only to certain forms of criminality.[2]

(ii) *Destitution*. When discussing the statistician-sociologists (see pp.53-5) we saw that it was discovered in the middle of the

[1] Dr. R. C. S. Kruyswyck-Hamburger, 'De resultaten van de opvoeding ingevolge de Kinderwetten' ('The results of education according to the Child Laws'), (*Mededeelingen van de Ned. Bond tot Kinderbescherming*, No. 25).

[2] The best criminological grouping of the various offences, is, I believe, the following: (i) the economic, i.e. having an economic motive, such as theft, fraud, procuring, and certain of the cases of arson and murder; (ii) the sexual, i.e. those with a sexual motive, as most of the 'moral' offences, but without procuring and such-like (iii) the aggressive, e.g. cruelty, damage to property, recalcitrance, manslaughter, certain cases of murder; therefore, most of the so-called 'personal' offences; and (iv) the political.

SOME ETIOLOGICAL RESULTS

nineteenth century that the curve of theft, etc., shows a rise when conditions in which the masses live become more difficult. The last and also the most important of the authors who have treated this aspect was G. von Mayr, who, in 1867, proved the relativity between theft and grain prices. These investigations have since been continued everywhere, as, for instance, in my own work *Criminality and economic conditions* (1915), in which I was able to produce the figures, showing this relation, for eighteen different countries. Since then, several other publications on the same subject have appeared. Among these were D. S. Thomas, *Social aspects of the business cycle* (1925); H. A. Phelps, *Cycles of crime*.[1] W. Woytinsky, in *Lebensmittelpreise, Beschäftigungsgrad und Kriminalität*,[2] and *Kriminalität und Lebensmittelpreise*[3]; Dr. J. Soudek, *Die sozialen Auswirkungen der Konjunkturschwankungen* (1929). I have myself set out the facts of this relation for the Netherlands elsewhere.[4] The most recent study in this field is Dr. E. Roesner's *Der Einfluss von Wirtschaftslage, Alkohol und Jahreszeit auf die Kriminalität* (1930), in which the most important and also the most recent literature is used and referred to. The following diagram is taken from this work.

GERMANY

The influence of prices and trade cycles on crime is unmistakable, in later times, as Germany becomes more industrialized —especially that of the trade cycle. The crisis years of 1891–2, 1901–2, and 1908–9 are especially notable for their high figures. Without wishing to deny that von Mayr's opinion as to the significance of what he calls 'objective Nahrungserschwerung' has some ground for justification, yet I believe that the 'subjective Nahrungserschwerung' (unemployment) is finally decisive.[5] Whoever has read through a good many

[1] *Journal of criminal law and criminology*, XX, 1929, p. 107.
[2] *Archiv für Sozialwissenschaft und Sozialpolitik*, B. 61, 1929, p. 21.
[3] *Zeitschrift für die gesammte Strafrechtswissenschaft*, B. 47, 1929.
[4] *De criminaliteit van Nederland* (*Criminality in the Netherlands*) Mensch en Maatschappij, VI, 1930, p. 230).
[5] Von Mayr overlooked that a sharp rise in grain prices causes

criminal records must have the conviction that unemployment is an extraordinarily important factor.

It has, therefore, been proved that the influence of destitution on economic criminality is very great; providing, of course, that one does not, quite arbitrarily, limit the concept 'destitution' to 'practical starvation'. It is, indeed, possible to give

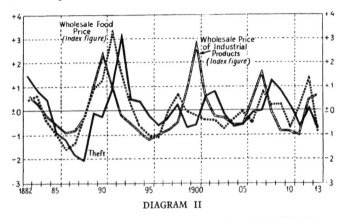

DIAGRAM II

THEFT, WHOLESALE FOOD PRICES, AND WHOLESALE PRICES OF
INDUSTRIAL PRODUCTS
(From E. Roesner, o.c., p. 22)

definite proof of this contention. Apart from the ups and downs caused by trade cycles the general trend of that particular kind of criminality which is more than any other caused by destitution, namely, simple theft, has been continually falling, which is in accordance with the decrease of poverty among the masses. Since the world war the care of the unemployed has greatly improved in most countries. The very severe economic crisis under which humanity is at present groaning is, accordingly, accompanied by a very much

restriction of purchasing power available for other goods, which in its turn creates unemployment. (*Vide*, about this, Woytinsky, *Lebensmittelpreise, Beschäftigungsgrad und Kriminalität* p. 52 et seq., also A. Loewe, *Arbeitslosigkeit und Kriminalität* (1914); and my own study *Verbrechen und Sozialismus* (*Neue Zeit*, XXX², 1912, p. 806).

smaller increase in theft than would undoubtedly have been the case in former times.

(iii) *Covetousness*. A number of criminologists recognize destitution as a sociological factor; but that which lies outside this limit—one might call it 'covetous criminality'[1]—many of them refuse to recognize as such; in that case, they say, we have to do with innate human tendencies, which we know it is difficult, if not impossible, to change.

Even to the merely superficially-trained in sociology it should be clear that this theory is erroneous. It is not denied that the possibility of these tendencies exists in human nature—there does not, indeed, exist any social fact which has not its corresponding psychic factor in man—but more than a possibility it is not. In one phase of social development one factor of human nature comes to full growth, and thereby to a primary place, and in different circumstances another. It is difficult for present-day humanity, with its powerful desires and urge for enjoyment, to imagine that in former periods this was totally different; although even now it is possible to ascertain—for instance, in remote agrarian parts, inhabited by small owner-farmers—that the mental make-up of the people may vary considerably, also in this respect.

As long as humanity has been divided into rich and poor—and this has been so for a very long time—the desires of the masses have been awakened by the display of wealth; only to be repressed again by the moral teaching impressed upon them, that this was a sinful thing. From the time of the French Revolution, however, all persons have been formally considered equals; and this last brake, therefore, has become continually weaker, and has now as good as disappeared. Covetousness has gripped the masses. It is only, however, for a small part —undoubtedly the very smallest part—that this can be

[1] Between the so-called 'destitution-offences' and the 'covetousness-offences' there are many intermediary cases. To deny, because of this, the existence of the two extreme groups would be just as foolish as to maintain that there is no difference between birds and mammals, because there exists an animal which forms a link between these two.

attributed to the contrast between wealth and poverty, especially since the wealthy are not so ostentatious as they used to be in former times. Another factor, grown ever more powerful, which now puts its stamp in absolute supremacy on the whole of life, has appeared on the scene since the middle of the nineteenth century. Large-scale investment capital has taken hold of the retail trade, employing every possible (and impossible) means to draw the attention of the people to its never-ending stream of goods. The big towns now have a social atmosphere of covetous desire forced up to the very top: Buy, buy more!—is shouted into the ears of the masses —there is plenty of everything! But many are not able to buy that which they desire so much—and with this we come to the criminological aspect of the matter.[1]

It is not apparent from criminal statistics from what motives a given offence was committed. Economic crimes are committed from destitution, from covetousness, and by professional criminals, but not in equal proportion. Simple theft is more usually committed from the first-named motive; embezzlement, falsification, and fraud more from the second, and qualified theft more generally by professional criminals. When comparing, for example, the trend of simple crime with that of fraud, one notices that the first-named offence is extremely sensitive to the trade cycle, the second only slightly; and further, that the trend of the movement is, for the first-named, directed downwards, and for the second, upwards. In other words, the decrease in destitution reduces the amount of crime of which it is the direct cause, whereas the ever-growing and awakening desires among the people create an increase in the particular kind of criminality which can be traced to them. The prognosis of this latter sort is not a favourable one.[2]

[1] One should not imagine that the things which are coveted, and to possess which thefts are committed, are something very wonderful; usually they are merely the most common things. Youths mostly steal so as to have plenty of cigarettes to smoke, and to go to the pictures; older people often in order to be able to go about with prostitutes.

[2] *Vide*, concerning this question, e.g. H. Trommer, *Urkundenfälschung und Betrug im Weltkriege* (1928); the relevant figures for the

SOME ETIOLOGICAL RESULTS

Next to the dynamic side of the problem we must mention the static. Embezzlement, obtaining money by false pretences, and fraud are offences which are mostly committed in the large towns. In the Netherlands (1923–27), 22·2 persons per 100,000 inhabitants were sentenced in the four largest municipalities for embezzlement, and 5·4 for obtaining money by false pretences; whereas these figures were, for the smaller municipalities (less than 5,000 inhabitants), 6·7 and 2·3 respectively.

(iv) *Sexual demoralization.* A very considerable proportion of sexual offences are actions on the part of individuals in whom sexuality has a merely physiological character, is not influenced in any way by other factors, and has not even been sublimated into erotics, which is the first level immediately above purely physical sexuality. Apart from serious pathological cases experience teaches us that every individual, even if born with a strong sexual urge, can be raised to this first level.

Now, numerous persons in present-day society grow up (conditions during youth are, undoubtedly, decisive in this respect) in an environment in which there is no question of any possible sublimation of sex life. The miserable housing conditions in which many of them live; the bad example, and the low mental standing of the parents are, in their case, the most important factors. At an age when they should be kept away from any sex-life, the children are brought into close touch with it. To name only one instance: from an inquiry held at Stuttgart it appeared that out of all the schoolchildren 33 per cent slept in crowded rooms, nearly 4 per cent had no bed, more than 50 per cent had no bed of their own, 6 per cent

Netherlands were reported by me in my *De criminaliteit van Nederland*. The first authors to draw attention to the part played by the large stores in criminality, and their significance for the etiology of crime were Lacassagne, *Les vols à l'étalage et dans les grands magasins* (Compte Rendu du IVe Congrès d'anthropologie criminelle), and P. Dubuisson, *Les voleuses des grands magasins* (Archives d'anthropologie criminelle, XVI). A more recent book is that by A. Antheaume *Le roman d'une épidémie Parisienne. Le vol à l'étalage* (undated, probably 1925).

slept with their parents in the same bed, and 6 per cent slept with a child of opposite sex.[1]

Finally, alcoholism plays some—if only a secondary—part in these matters. The following remarks relate to this aspect of the question.

(v) *Alcoholism* is related to crime in three ways: (1) by way of heredity (vitiation of the embryo), which will not be dealt with in this book; (2) chronic alcoholism; and (3) acute intoxication.

Chronic alcoholism causes a general weakening of the mental functions, more especially the moral ones. The sufferer frequently becomes irritable and jealous, sometimes loses his sense of shame, neglects his work, and thereby gets at low ebb. All kinds of crime are the consequence of this.[2]

Since 1878, when the first work on alcoholism appeared from the pen of A. Baer, who ascertained a percentage of 19·2 of chronic drinkers among the detained in German prisons,[3] numerous publications on the subject have made their appearance, all of which confirm that the number of these people among criminals is considerable. In my own work, *Criminality and economic conditions*, I reported on this matter at length.[4] I will confine myself to giving a few figures from the Netherlands Criminal Statistics (1901-5), as elaborated by Th. van der Woude.[5] (See Table III.)

We see that the significance of chronic alcoholism is, for some offences, important; when combined with drunkenness, even extremely so.[6] The highest percentage (begging and vagrancy, 33·7 per cent) is probably still too low. H. T. de Graaf, in his work *Karakter en behandeling van veroordeelden wegens landlooperij en bedelarij* (1914) (*Character and treatment*

[1] *Vide* Gruhle, t.a.p., p. 109.
[2] *Vide*, concerning this, the very important study by A. Ley and R. Charpentier, *Alcoholisme et criminalité* (1910), Ch. III, p. 43 et seq.
[3] *Der Alcoholismus*, p. 348.
[4] p. 508 et seq.
[5] *De Wegwijzer*, XVIII, 1915, p. 3 et seq.
[6] The Criminal Statistics for 1911-15 and for 1919 contain more recent data. The relative percentages, have, generally speaking, decreased.

TABLE III

Crimes and slight non-indictable offences	Total number of persons sentenced	Chronic alcoholists		Chronic and occasional alcoholists	
		Absolute	Per cent	Absolute	Per cent
Economic:					
Simple larceny	7,210	984	13·6	1,449	20·1
Aggravated larceny	4,170	370	8·8	581	13·9
Embezzlement	1,502	220	14·6	300	19·9
Fraud, obtaining by false pretences	467	79	16·9	93	19·9
Begging and vagrancy	8,300	2,803	33·7	2,845	34·3
Sexual:					
Pubic indecency	437	37	8·4	107	24·5
Rape, etc.	649	53	8·1	115	17·9
Aggressive:					
Simple assault	16,569	1,919	11·5	6,752	40·7
Aggravated assault	1,987	350	17·6	1,148	59·3
Assaults on officials	5,371	1,308	24·3	3,919	72·9
Breach of domestic peace	1,268	225	17·6	751	29·2

of persons sentenced for vagrancy and begging), reports that 66·1 per cent of these detained people were big, and 26·8 per cent fairly big drinkers.[1] In this connexion we should, of course, not forget that the causality may also be the other way round (this is especially so in the case of begging and vagrancy), in the sense that their criminal career has led to alcoholism.

Besides an investigation into the number of chronic alcoholists among criminals, it is also of importance to trace the number of crimes of which habitual drinkers are found guilty. The Chief of the 'Medical Consultation Bureau for Alcoholism' at Amsterdam, Th. van der Woude, gives in this connexion the following figures: out of 765 patients, 549 or 71·7 per cent were known to the police (i.e. had been prosecuted for some offence or other).[2] The following table gives some information concerning the nature and frequency of the offences committed by them. (See Table IV).

Criminality among chronic alcoholists is, as we see from these figures, extensive and of great variety. These figures have, moreover, been confirmed from other sources. E. G. Dresel reports, concerning a number of habitual drinkers examined by him in an asylum for inebriates at Heidelberg, that out of 151 there were 108, or 71·5 per cent who were known to the police, and that these latter had between them 858 sentences—i.e. an average of eight per head![3]

Acute alcoholism has very little significance in the case of economic criminality (without 'Dutch courage' burglars would probably do their 'work' just the same); but in sexual criminality it plays some, and in aggressive crime a very important part. Proofs of this contention are abundantly available. A few may here suffice.[4]

[1] p. 144.
[2] 'Delicten bij de patienten van het Medisch Consultatie Bureau voor Alcoholisme (*De Wegwijzer*, XVIII, 1915) ('Offences among the Patients of the Medical Consultation Bureau for Alcoholism').
[3] 'Die Ursachen der Trunksucht und ihre Bekämpfung durch die Trinkerfürsorge in Heidelberg' (1921).
[4] In my *Criminality and economic conditions* I have dealt with the connexion in question (*vide*, p. 619–20 and 639 et seq.). Also later, in a separate publication, *Dronkenschapsdelicten van criminologisch*

TABLE IV

Crimes and slight non-indictable offences	Number of persons sentenced	Number of persons from Col. 2, also sentenced for:										
		I	II	III	IV	V	VI	VII	VIII	IX	X	Total
I. Drunkenness	432	—	88	20	5	2	4	6	59	13	38	235
II. Assault on officials	124	88	—	14	6	3	3	3	29	5	14	165
III. Assault	33	20	14	—	1	1	1	1	3	2	2	45
IV. Insulting language	7	5	6	1	—	1	0	0	2	0	1	16
V. Intimidation	3	2	3	1	1	—	0	0	1	0	1	9
VI. Malicious damage	4	4	3	1	0	0	—	0	1	1	3	13
VII. Sexual offences	18	6	3	1	0	0	0	—	1	0	1	12
VIII. Larceny	110	59	29	3	2	1	1	1	—	4	9	109
IX. Embezzlement	24	13	5	2	0	0	1	0	4	—	2	27
X. Begging and vagrancy	43	38	14	2	1	1	3	1	9	1	—	70

Firstly, as regards *sexual criminality*. Alcohol enhances—at any rate, in the first stages of inebriation—the libido, and weakens the 'brakes', i.e. the power of the individual to check himself. The percentage of sexual offences committed under the influence of alcohol is, generally, somewhere in the neighbourhood of 10 per cent for the Netherlands; for offences against public decency (1901–5) it was 21 per cent; in 1919 it amounted to 11·4; for the remaining sexual offences in 1901–5, 13·4 per cent, and in 1919, 7·5 per cent.[1]

These percentages are not high, alcohol having in these cases a merely secondary importance. This is confirmed by the trend of these offences, which was, up to the war, somewhat, and since the close of the war, strongly on the upgrade, whereas the consumption of alcohol has fallen considerably during the same period.[2]

The connexion between *aggressive criminality* and drunkenness is, physiologically as well as psychologically, easily traceable: alcohol enhances the tendency to mobility, which easily gives rise to all sorts of conflicts; it increases irritability and weakens self-control. The causality may be ascertained in different ways. In the first place by the direct method; how many offenders were under the influence of strong drink at the time of the action? For a number of countries the relevant figures are available. Without exception the percentages given are high, in some countries even very high, e.g. Sweden (1908), where 64 per cent of cases of assault upon constables, 74 per cent of wounding, 84 per cent of breaches of domestic peace, and 85 per cent of the murders are committed in drunkenness! The figures for the Netherlands were, from

standpunt bezien (De Wegwijzer, XVIII, 1915), (*Strong drink offences viewed from criminological standpoint*) where an extensive bibliography is given.

[1] *Vide* Th. van de Woude, 'Alcohol en zedelijkheids-delict' (*De Wegwijzer*, XVII) ('Alcohol and moral delict'), and 'Alcohol en misdaad', 1936 ('Alcohol and crime'), the most exhaustive monograph which has been published so far on this matter; see also the Criminal Statistics for 1919.

[2] *Vide*, concerning this, e.g. my *De criminaliteit van Nederland*, p. 242 et seq.

TABLE V[1]

Offences	Persons sentenced, who, at the time they committed the offence, were under the influence of alcohol											
	Including habitual drunkards							Excluding habitual drunkards				
	1910		1915		1919		1910		1915		1919	
	Absolute	Per cent	Absolute	Per cent	Absolute	Per cent	Absolute	Per cent	Absolute	Per cent	Absolute	Per cent
Assaults and other offences against officials	1,119	54·7	898	54·8	416	39·6	775	45·5	688	48·1	287	31·2
Simple assault	1,162	34·4	794	30·6	400	21·0	928	29·5	635	26·1	302	16·7
Murder, manslaughter, and aggravated assault	57	49·1	39	42·8	17	23·9	43	42·1	26	33·3	12	18·8

[1] Reprinted from the *Criminal Statistics for 1919*, pp. XXIV-XXV.

1901–5, as follows: malicious damage 47 per cent, slight assault 36 per cent, aggravated assault 55 per cent, and assault upon constables 69 per cent.

These percentages still remain fairly high, even when alcoholism is later reduced to smaller proportions; but they are nevertheless noticeably smaller, while the absolute figures are considerably lower. The next table gives the relevant facts for the Netherlands. (See Table V.)

Besides the direct method, there are indirect ways in which the connexion in question may be ascertained; i.e. by means of geographical comparison, or by comparing criminality among different groups of the population, where alcohol consumption differs considerably (Statica). We have also the dynamic investigation method, a single instance of which may be cited.[1]

Aggressive criminality occurs to a widely-divergent extent on different days of the week; and in view of the fact that it is on Sundays that most alcohol is consumed it may be useful to look up the relevant facts and figures. In the following Table a few of these have been collected. (See Table VI.)

The percentages for the Sunday move between about thirty and sixty, so that, roughly speaking, one may say that about half of these offences are committed on that day.

Finally, a few words about the curve of alcohol consumption. Alcoholism, as a national disease, prevailed for a great part of the nineteenth century in the most violent form, a scourge to the masses. During the latter part of the century —earlier in one country than in the other; in Germany, for example, not until the commencement of the twentieth century—a revulsion set in, and alcohol-consumption began to decrease. In the Netherlands, it amounted to about 10 litres of spirits in 1880 per head of the population, whereas now it is only about 2·5 litres per head per year! Greater prosperity and culture among the masses, who have awakened

[1] The whole of this matter was dealt with exhaustively in my above-mentioned study *Dronkenschapsdelicten*, etc.

SOME ETIOLOGICAL RESULTS 103

out of their misery and mental coma, have wrought this great change.[1]

If it is true that alcoholism is such an important factor in the etiology of aggressive criminality, then it should follow that the latter has decreased during later years. This is, indeed, a fact. To name only a single instance: in the Netherlands, from the beginning of the present century until the

TABLE VI[2]

	Percentages of assault and manslaughter on the different days of the week						
	Vienna 1896–7	Korneuburg 1896–7	Zürich 1890	Düsseldorf	Worms 1896–8	Heidelberg 1900–4	Straubing 1900–9
Sunday	29·8	51·8	42·5	56·3	38·8	45·0	63·0
Monday	21·5	8·6	15·6	14·9	15·6	16·3	
Tuesday	11·9	7·9		4·2	9·3	8·5	
Wednesday	8·3	10·1	29·1	4·2	9·3	6·0	37·0
Thursday	8·3	10·8		2·3	9·5	5·5	
Friday	7·9	2·9		1·8	7·4	7·3	
Saturday	12·3	7·9	12·8	16·3	10·1	8·4	
Total	100·0	100·0	100·0	100·0	100·0	100·0	100·0

'thirties, assaults on officials decreased, roughly, from about 20 per 100,000 of the population to about 13; ordinary assault from nearly 70 to under 50, and qualified assault from about 8 to a little over 3!

[1] It would take me too far, in this little work, to go into the social causes of alcoholism as well. I refer in this connexion to my *Criminality and economic conditions* (p. 357 et seq.), where the most important literature on this question is also mentioned.
[2] Reprinted from my *Dronkenschapsdelicten*, etc.

(vi) *Lack of culture.* However important alcoholism may be as a factor in criminal violence, there is another necessary element, namely lack of culture and refinement, and consequent lack of self-control. Whereas this was at one time the general fate of the masses, during the last fifty years they have attained a higher level in this respect also. Nevertheless, there are still large groups, living in the most miserable spiritual state, to whom culture is a mere word—barbarism in the midst of cultured society. It is therefore not to be wondered at that the most backward countries, districts, and groups of the population show the highest figures of aggressive criminality. To mention only one fact: in Germany the figures for aggravated assault are, among intellectuals, about 25 per 100,000 of the population; among persons working in industry about 500, and among unskilled labourers 1,680![1]

(vii) *War.* Students of the physical sciences are, for various reasons, being envied by their colleagues of the social sciences, one of the reasons being that they always have the experimental method at their disposal, while sociologists have to do without this. On very rare occasions, however, Fate has smiled on the latter by creating a situation, which—although not an experiment, as it was not purposely created with this intention—yet amounted to much the same thing. One instance of such a situation is war—this being one of the very rare occasions on which we are able to say something to the credit of this terrible scourge of humanity. Now, the war has driven up to the top almost all the factors which may lead to crime. Family life was torn asunder through the absence of the man and the outdoor labour of the married woman; large numbers of children were being neglected; sexual demoralization was another consequence; poverty and destitution played havoc with the population, chiefly in those countries which were hit by the blockade, and the high value of certain articles increased the incentive to wrong-doing; the urge to enjoyment and covetousness had humanity, which groaned under so

[1] About this matter, *vide Criminality and economic conditions*, p. 630 et seq.

SOME ETIOLOGICAL RESULTS 105

much accumulated suffering, in its grip; general demoralization prevailed throughout the war, with its killing and maiming, its terrible destruction, its requisitioning or whatever it is called; all of which was completely opposed to the morals of normal life.

The proofs of our contention are available: the facts of the 'experiment' tally with the theory. The statistics show criminality to have swollen like a avalanche, but in reality it increased much more still. For a large part of the male population, at the most criminal age, was in military service, and thereby outside the jurisdiction of the ordinary courts (the figures of the crimes committed in the field will probably never be published); while owing to the weakening of the police and justiciary staffs a considerably smaller number of offences was discovered and prosecuted. Only minimum figures are therefore available.

We shall mention a single instance only: In Austria, total criminality rose from just over 9,000 sentences in 1913 to over 11,000 in 1918, and to more than 31,000 in 1921; one of the features of the beginning of the War being, everywhere, a decreasing criminality. Especially economic crimes increased: i.e. theft, in 1913, 3,610; in 1916, 4,375; in 1918, 9,118; in 1920, 26,050.[1] In Germany, economic criminality among the civil population rose, in the case of theft, from about 40,000 persons sentenced in 1914, to about 106,000 in 1918; while general criminality amounted to about 460,000 in 1914, and rose in the period following the War (1923) to about 954,000.[2] In the Netherlands, the number of condemned persons rose from 13,424 (i.e. 21·8 per 10,000 of the population) in 1913, to 23,033 (33·8) in 1919; e.g. theft rose from 33·0 per 100,000 in 1914, to 102·7 in 1919, an increase of 210 per cent.[3]

[1] *Vide* F. Exner, *Krieg und Kriminalität in Oesterreich* (1927), p. 24. One should place increases such as these, side by side with Lombroso's theory, according to which crime is inborn!
[2] *Vide* M. Liepmann, *Krieg und Kriminalität in Deutschland* (1930), pp. 15 and 58. Liepmann's book contains an extensive bibliography.
[3] *Vide* my own *De Criminaliteit van Nederland*. About the Netherlands, *vide* also De Roos and Suermondt, 'Die Kriminalität in den Niederlanden während und nach dem Kriege' (*Monatschrift für*

20. PHYSICAL ENVIRONMENT

The influence of natural surroundings (climate, soil, etc.) on man and society has been realized from the times of antiquity. Thus, Herodotus (489–34) points to the influence of the Nile floods in Egyptian history; Hippocrates (460–377) attributed the cowardice of the Oriental to the hot climate; Strabo (64–19) relates the pacifism of peoples living in open plains to their physical environment. In the sixteenth century, the French jurist and historian, J. Bodin (1530–96), takes up these ideas again; and Montesquieu (1689–1755) uses them as one of the foundations of his book *Esprit des Lois* (1748). He even makes a distinction in principle between the direct and indirect influences of these circumstances.

The direct influences—especially climate—have an immediate effect on man, e.g. on his sexual inclinations; while the indirect ones—especially the soil—are of importance for man *via* society; an instance of which is the necessity of insuring irrigation, which, in the East, gave rise to despotism. As far as I am aware, Montesquieu was the first author who saw the possible significance of this theory for criminology.

'You will find in northern climes people who have few vices, sufficient virtues, much sincerity and frankness. Turn to the lands of the south, you will think yourself journeying away from morality itself: more violent passions will multiply crimes: each man will seek to take all the advantages over others which can favour these same crimes. In temperate countries you will see people less determined in their

Kriminal-Psychologie und Strafrechtsform, XIV, 1923). About France, Belgium, England, Italy, and Roumania, P. Yocas, *L'influence de la guerre européenne sur la criminalité* (1926); about Sweden and Norway, O. Grönlund, 'Ueber die Kriminalitat in neutralen Ländern (Schweden und Norwegen) wahrend der Kriegs- und Nach-kriegszeit' (*Monatschrift für Kriminalpyschologie und Strafrechtsreform*, XVI, 1925), about Czecho-Slovakia, Solnar 'La guerre mondiale et la criminalité en Tschécoslovaque (*Revue de droit pénal et de criminologie*, IX, p. 858). In England, criminality has not, on the whole, had an unfavourable course.

PHYSICAL ENVIRONMENT 107

behaviour, even in their vices and their virtues: the climate is not sufficiently definite to make the people themselves definite.'[1]

Other writers of the eighteenth century as, for example, Turgot (1717–81), Hume (1711–76), and Ferguson (1723–1816), while recognizing the importance of this theory, do not think it as great as does Montesquieu. Herder (1744–1803) is the most important among those who have pursued this environment theory; for some time after this it occupies a less prominent place, only to come to the fore again, however, in the second half of the nineteenth century, in the writings of Taine (1828–93), and especially in those of Buckle (1821–62). The greatest personality among the moderns, in this field, is the German anthropo-geographist, F. Ratzel (1844–1904). Stripped of its exaggerations, the doctrine of physical environment still plays an important part in sociology and anthropology.

It is not surprising that this theory has gradually won for itself some place in criminology also. Among other writers, Quetelet,[2] Lacassagne,[3] Ferri, von Liszt, Aschaffenburg,[4] Gaedeken,[5] and Roesner,[6] have paid attention to it. We shall now deal with some of its chief points.

The indirect influences, i.e. those which take their effect via society, will not here be considered. The birth of industrialism in England, for example, is undoubtedly closely related to the presence of iron and coal below the earth's surface; but to attribute the enormous increase in criminality in those days to this physical fact is surely to trace the thread of causality

---

[1] *Esprit des lois*, B. XIV, Chapter II.
[2] *Physique sociale*, Livre IV, Chapter II, pp. 4 and 5.
[3] 'Marche de la criminalité en France', 1825–80 (*Revue Scientifique*, 1881).
[4] *Das Verbrechen und seine Bekämpfung*, I. Teil, p 15 (3rd ed.).
[5] 'Contribution statistique à la réaction de l'organisme sous l'influence physicochimique des agents météorologiques' (*Archives d'anthropologie criminelle*, XXIV, 1909).
[6] *Der Einfluss von Wirtschaftslage, Alcohol und Jahreszeit auf die Kriminalität* (1930), p. 69 et seq.

somewhat too far back. On the same line of reasoning one might say that the inventor of gunpowder was the cause of all the crimes committed by means of firearms!

We shall trace, for the various kinds of crime in succession, the direct relation to which we have referred, both statically and dynamically. Before doing so we may mention that the direct influence of climate, etc., is getting smaller, owing to the development of scientific technique and the consequent power over the forces of nature which man is able to exercise in ever-growing measure.

(i) *Economic criminality*. For various reasons, which we have already mentioned, there are serious objections to international comparison by means of criminal statistics. Notwithstanding this, and with all possible reserve, it may be thought probable that Southern Europe has less economic criminality than Northern Europe. As far as what is called 'destitution-crime' is concerned, this must surely be traced to the smaller needs of the population in respect of food, housing, and clothing. This influence, however, is of quite a secondary character, because the effect of the greater needs which the northern climate entails may easily be neutralized by provident social measures. The low 'covetous' criminality in the south has nothing whatever to do with physical environment, but is entirely dependent upon the fact that the northern part is in a much higher phase of industrial development than the southern. In the thirteenth, fourteenth, and fifteenth centuries it is therefore likely that the facts of criminality were the other way round.

The dynamical aspect of the matter is of no importance so far as the years are concerned. We have previously seen (p. 90, et seq.) that economic criminality varies with wholesale grain prices and trade cycles. There is no connexion whatever between this movement and such things as changes of temperature, etc., unless it be in an extremely remote connexion, e.g. *via* larger or smaller crops. The monthly movements of these offences is very marked: they increase strongly towards the autumn, culminating in the winter, after which they decrease again towards the spring, reaching their lowest point in the summer.

The explanation of this course of things is quite simple: the curve of unemployment, which has been added in Diagram III, speaks volumes in this respect. The lighter forms

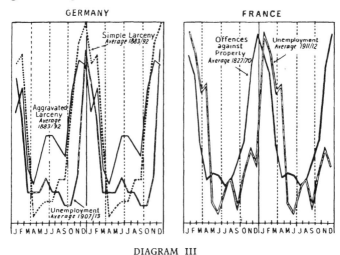

DIAGRAM III
THE COURSE OF ECONOMIC CRIMINALITY IN GERMANY AND FRANCE
FOR THE VARIOUS MONTHS OF THE YEAR
(Reprinted from Roesner, o.c., p. 71)

of economic criminality rise and fall most markedly; the more serious forms—which are to a large extent committed by professional criminals—less so. Qualified theft (burglary, etc.) shows a secondary climax in the summer, which may be explained by the fact of many houses standing empty during this time.

Roesner's curves are very eloquent indeed; but they make no mention of any figures. We therefore reproduce, in Table VII, the figures for Germany, including those for other kinds of offences, for the years 1883–92. (See Table VII).

(ii) *Sexual criminality.* It is not possible to make any

reliable pronouncement in regard to international comparativity of this form of criminality. I am under the impression that the amount of sexual criminality which has been ascertained in Southern Europe is somewhat greater than in Northern Europe; but this is merely an impression. Should this be so, then the possibility exists that it is a result of a greater assertiveness of the sexual urge under the influence of the climate. I believe, however, that so little is definitely known concerning this that this aspect of the problem cannot here be dealt with further.

Concerning the dynamics of these offences adequate information is available. From Table VII it is clear that there is a sharp rise from January to July—from 64 to 149; i.e. 85, or 132 per cent! When shown diagrammatically, we get the following picture (see p. 112, Diagram IV).

The first observation which these figures and curves lead us to make is that the increase has already started before there is any question of a noticeable rise in temperature—let alone of warmth. It is therefore probable that in this respect another factor is more important, namely, the lengthening of the days and the better weather. A large proportion of sexual criminality is opportunist crime (quiet roads, etc.), and is therefore less frequent in winter-time.

The second observation is that sexual offences are naturally committed more in the open air in the spring and summer, and therefore more likely to be detected; in other words, the actual increase is probably less than the figures would lead one to suspect.

The remainder of the rise is probably connected with an enhanced sexual urge, which is also expressed in the higher figures of conception. In this connexion a few remarks may not be out of place. In the first place, the conception figures for children born in wedlock do not show a rise in February and March, but only in April; in the second place, the maximum lies in May, and not, as in the case of sexual crime, in July; and in the third place, the course of this curve does not show the sharp rises and falls of that of the sexual offences.

TABLE VII. GERMANY[1]

If, during the year, 100 offences are committed, on an average, every day, then this will be, in one day, for the months of:

Offences	January	February	March	April	May	June	July	August	September	October	November	December
Simple larceny	113	115	98	85	87	88	88	92	92	106	117	121
Aggravated larceny	102	107	92	89	94	98	98	94	96	106	112	111
Embezzlement	100	97	94	94	98	100	103	101	98	104	105	108
Fraud	112	108	95	88	92	92	92	93	90	88	102	121
Sexual crimes	64	66	78	103	128	144	149	130	108	90	68	69
Assault on officials	89	94	89	94	97	104	109	117	112	104	99	90
Insulting language	83	89	85	93	108	115	120	122	113	99	93	80
Malicious damage	88	92	98	108	109	106	104	104	103	101	99	88
Breach of domestic peace	94	99	96	100	98	101	105	110	106	102	100	89
Simple assault	76	80	79	95	108	116	124	134	121	102	88	74
Aggravated assault	75	78	78	95	108	113	118	133	124	106	93	78

[1] Reprinted from G. Aschaffenburg, *Das Verbrechen und seine Bekämpfung* (1923), 3rd edition, p. 16.

112   THE FRENCH SCHOOL

The maximum and minimum do not deviate more than about 10 per cent, whereas, for the conception curve of illegitimate children, this figure is 31 per cent. In other words, the natural enhancement of the sexual urge towards the spring is

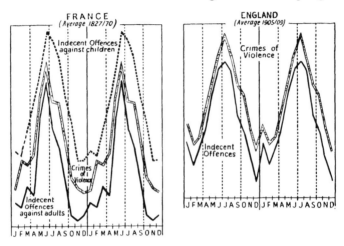

DIAGRAM IV

THE COURSE OF SEXUAL AND AGGRESSIVE CRIMINALITY IN FRANCE
AND ENGLAND FOR THE VARIOUS MONTHS OF THE YEAR
(Taken from Roesner, o.c., p. 71)

felt by married people, i.e. those who have regular sexual intercourse, much less than by others. This, among other things, explains the sharp rise in sexual criminality—which is committed to a large extent by unmarried people.

(iii) *Aggressive criminality.* As far as statics are concerned it is certain that this form of criminality is greater in the southern countries of Europe than in the northern—this, however, is not to say that it is still greater as we approach still nearer to the equator, nor that it has always been the same in earlier phases of social development.[1] (See Table VIII.)

[1] Compare G. Tarde, 'Géographie criminelle', in *La criminalité comparée*.

PHYSICAL ENVIRONMENT 113

The principal reason for these great differences is probably to be found in the totally different stage of culture in which these countries live, and which is reflected in the illiteracy figures. The differences within Italy, for example, are

TABLE VIII[1]

Countries	Years	Murder and assault, resulting in death, per 100,000 inhabitants	Years	Illiteracy Per cent
Italy	1880–84	70·0	1882	57·4
Spain	1883–84	64·9	1889	68·1
Hungary	1876–80	56·2	1880	59·7
Austria	1877–81	10·8	,,	40·1
Belgium	1876–80	8·5	,,	21·6
Ireland	1880–84	8·1	1882	30·0
France	,,	6·4	,,	13·1
Scotland	,,	4·4	,,	11·0
England	,,	3·9	1883	14·0
Germany	1882–84	3·4	1881–82	1·54
Holland	1880–81	3·1	1880	11·5

greater than those between Italy as a whole and the countries at the bottom of the list. Sicily, for instance, has a murder figure of 36·5 per 100,000 inhabitants, and Parma only 1·1! This, of course, is not to say that neither climate nor race has anything to do with these differences, as is shown by the great deviations in the curve for the different months. With this we have arrived at the dynamic aspect of the phenomenon.

We have already seen from Table VII that this sort of crime

[1] Reprinted from *Criminality and economic conditions*, p. 631. These figures have fallen considerably since that time; generally speaking, the order of sequence has not altered much. *Vide* E. Roy Calvert, *Capital punishment in the twentieth century* (1927).

reaches its minimum in the winter, after which it rises fairly regularly, until it reaches its maximum in July-August. This is shown clearly in the next graph.

Ferri attributes this increase chiefly to the physiological effect of the heat, which leaves a larger surplus of energy; to the better nourishment of the population in the summer, and

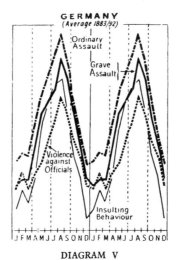

DIAGRAM V

THE COURSE OF AGGRESSIVE CRIMINALITY IN GERMANY FOR THE
VARIOUS MONTHS OF THE YEAR
(Taken from Roesner, p. 70)

to an enhanced irritability.[1] Now the first two reasons given by him seem to me to be entirely illusory. These kinds of offences are not committed because one is fed better, nor are they refrained from because one is less well fed: the best-fed people commit the smallest number of violent crimes. I should say that the most important cause of the rise lies in the fact that in summer the people drink more alcohol, and come

[1] 'Das Verbrechen in seiner Abhängigkeit von dem jährlichen Temperaturwechsel' (*Zeitschrift für die gesammte Strafrechtswissenschaft*, II).

more into contact with each other. Besides, as we have already seen and as the figures and diagrams indicate, the rise has already begun in the months when there is not yet any sign of warmth—while, on the other hand, the days begin to lengthen. An adequate proof that Ferri's theory in this respect is erroneous lies in the trend of these offences through the days of the week (see Table VI, p. 103). There is, of course, no reason whatever to suppose that the temperature is always very high on Sundays—though, admittedly, the arguments may, at times, be somewhat heated.

The principal explanation of this monthly dynamics lies in the changing social conditions, which in their turn are influenced by physical environment. Whether the whole problem is thereby solved I should not, however, be prepared to say. The possibility exists that the change of season increases people's (or rather, some people's) irritability. In this connexion it is significant that both suicide and insanity also increase during this time of the year.

In any case, the matter has not yet been fully cleared up; and perhaps a special inquiry into the proportionate amount of criminal violence on very hot days would shed the necessary light on it.

(iv) *Political criminality*. This need not detain us long. Lombroso and Laschi, authors of *Il delitto politico e le revoluzioni* (1890), produce in that book a map showing Germany and Russia as the countries with the least revolutions! We should not say that now!

The connexion between political crime and climate, etc., is a highly improbable one. Revolutions occur when social development clashes with political institutions which do not possess enough elasticity. Such things as attempts to kill high personages arise from a complexity of social factors in which climate plays no part whatever.

In the same work some graphs are printed, according to which more revolutions occur in the spring and summer than in other seasons. The explanation of this is probably that in those seasons people are more out of doors, and therefore sooner form into crowds. But that by itself would hardly be sufficient to start a revolution!

On surveying the whole of the data at our disposal it is clear that the importance of physical environment for the etiology of crime, if it exists at all, is of a very secondary nature. As von Liszt once expressed it: 'We no longer believe in any *fauna* or *flora criminalis* produced by certain climatic or geological conditions.'[1]

[1] 'Die sozialpolitische Auffassung des Verbrechens' (*Sozialpolitisches Centralblatt*, 1892, p. 4).

CHAPTER VI

THE BIO-SOCIOLOGICAL SCHOOL

WHEN speaking of Ferri (see p. 76) we pointed out that it is to him that we owe the synthesis of the anthropological and environment theories. His formula is: *every crime is a product of individual, social, and physical factors*. What is meant here by 'individual factors' is those which were analysed and explained by Lombroso.

In the course of time a good many criminologists have gone over to this way of thinking; and one may say, indeed, that it has become the prevailing trend of thought. Amongst others, the founders of the Union Pénale Internationale, Ad. Prins (1845–1919) of Brussels, Fr. von Liszt (1851–1919), of Berlin, and G. A. van Hamel (1842–1917) of Amsterdam, should be ranked among the adherents of this school—von Liszt at a later age inclining more and more towards the sociological side. We may further mention as belonging to the same group the German criminologists G. Aschaffenburg (1866), and E. Wulffen (1862), and also the Dutch criminal law jurist D. Simons (1860–1930).

21. CRITICAL EXAMINATION

The formula: every crime = individual + environment factors is, when taken literally, correct; i.e. with the emphasis on 'every'. Any given crime, taken separately, is the product of these two factors. The formula has also the curious merit of applying to all human actions—both criminal and non-criminal. At bottom, all it amounts to is this: men are not equal, not in any respect—which is one of the reasons why their actions differ so much.

Before proceeding to examine what is the significance of this formula for criminal sociology it is essential to point out that the individual factor, at the time the action is committed, consists of two sub-factors. These are, firstly, the circumstances which have influenced the individual from birth, down to the time of the action; and secondly, his individual propensities. After what has been explained before—in Chapter V —it need not be stressed here that this first environment-factor is of an extraordinarily great importance; it is, indeed, more often than not the deciding one. Ferri's formula should, therefore, really be amended as follows: every crime = (environment + propensities) + environment. Environment has, indeed, always a twofold effect on a human being.

In this limited sense the formula is correct, even when one takes Ferri's contention—that of two persons, living and having lived in exactly the same unfavourable circumstances, sometimes only one becomes a criminal—at its face value. This, of course, is merely a hypothetical case, as no two persons ever live and have lived in *exactly* the same circumstances. Slight differences, e.g. in environment during infancy, may sometimes be the cause of very great differences later in life.

Now what is the nature of this individual factor? Ferri, in concordance with Lombroso's views, says it is a pathological one; at first he also held it to be atavistic. We have previously seen (p. 60, et seq.) that this hypothesis is untenable. The majority of criminals are physically and mentally quite sound. The solution of the problem, as stated by Ferri and others, is far simpler than he imagines, far more matter-of-fact. It has, however, the advantage of being correct.

Let us start from the supposition that two people actually live and have lived in precisely the same circumstances; that both of them, let us say, have an opportunity of committing a very advantageous crime, and that neither of the two has any objections of a moral nature. At the decisive moment we should see that the one has the pluck to do the deed, while the other funks it, and retires. So courage is a factor of crime, and cowardice of virtue? Indeed, this often happens. Or, maybe, the one is sharp enough to see the great danger of

CRITICAL EXAMINATION 119

being discovered, and refrains from the action, leaving the fool to commit it. So therefore craftiness is a factor of virtue, and stupidity of vice? Indeed this, too, is an everyday occurrence. The opposite, of course, happens as well; neither Thérèse Humbert, nor Alberti, Hatry, or Kreuger, would have been able to commit their grandiose frauds unless they had been exceptionally intelligent. As a matter of fact, nobody who has a slight criminological training would consider the professional criminal stupid.

In other words, all possible kinds of quite ordinary human qualities may either lead a man to crime, or keep him away from it. That depends upon many different circumstances. Even the quality which might naturally be expected to lead to crime before any other, i.e. lack of moral sense, is not one which is exclusively connected with the commitment of crime. For, this very same quality, providing its bearer is sensible and capable enough—and providing circumstances allow him—to avoid going beyond the border-line of criminal law, may lead to great successes in life. A certain proportion of criminals belong to the most dangerous and harmful class of people in existence (the majority are more troublesome than dangerous), but it is a totally mistaken idea to imagine that these are the only ones belonging to that category: there are also grandiose scoundrels in the non-juridical, and merely moral sense. The most ordinary experience of life (which one does not gather in a laboratory) can teach us that.

Ferri's famous question: how is it, that in a given unfavourable set of circumstances out of two individuals only one becomes a criminal?—Winkler called this question the Achilles-heel of the environment-theory—must be answered as follows: *because one man possesses some human quality which in itself has nothing, or need not have anything, to do with crime, to a greater degree than another man.*

Manouvrier once expressed this as follows:

'All things being equal some people have more disposition to crime than others. Of course! Just as man is more disposed to crime than woman, as the man who is robust and bold is more disposed to crimes of violence than the man who is weedy and timid, etc., although, on the whole, every physical type finds some kind of crime practicable, be it only arson. The athlete will be more liable to strike, the fine talker to swindle, but for that reason we shall not stamp either strength, eloquence, boldness, agility, or cleverness as criminal'.[1]

In other words, predisposition to crime—as to all other actions—varies considerably in different people. Who, among environment-theorists, would deny this? What they do deny, however, is that this predisposition is, in the majority of cases, of a special character; while they also point out that this tendency only leads to crime in certain special circumstances.

The formula: a given, separate, crime = individual + social factors—which in itself is correct—must not be loosely extended to: 'criminality as a social mass-phenomenon = individual + social factors'; because, in that way, human factors which, in themselves, have nothing whatever to do with criminality, and which under different circumstances might lead to totally different conduct, are stamped as factors in criminality.

It is clear what the objection to the above will be; and it has been stated frequently enough. That is all very well—it is said—but it does not make any difference to the fact that, if in that one special case this predisposition—no matter whether it was in itself of a criminal character—had not been present, there would at any rate have been one crime less. Should it, therefore, so happen that this occurs in the mass, then mass-criminality would also have been less.

To this objection—which is an erroneous one—I may be permitted to reply with a few final remarks. I must first, however, point out that the results of criminal statistics would be completely incomprehensible if, accidentally, large numbers of individuals showing certain characteristics to a very

[1] *La genèse normale du crime*, p. 451.

marked degree, were born at certain times, and none at others. For it is precisely one of the things which these statistics teach us that, unless extraordinary events come into play (crises, war, etc.), criminality recurs from year to year with the greatest regularity. Fundamentally, the regularly and similarly-returning distribution of human inclinations and propensities is one of the postulates of criminal sociology; and, as a matter of fact, of the science of sociology as a whole.

22. THE LAW OF INDIVIDUAL VARIATIONS

It is a matter of ancient experience that individuals of the same species—including man—vary in every respect. No two leaves of a tree are identical, let alone two individuals of the most complex being, *homo sapiens*. This variability is apparently entirely chaotic; when one looks at any ordinary crowd of people, it is not possible to observe any sign of regularity in, for example, their height. Until the beginning of the nineteenth century it was, indeed, believed that these individual variations were quite chaotic. It was, however, shown then that this was only apparently so.

The same investigator who was the first to notice the regularity in the trend of criminality—the Belgian statistician Ad. Quetelet—discovered that there is a strict lawfulness which governs individual variations in human beings. When one arranges a number of people, e.g. according to their height, and one draws a line along the tops of their heads, one notices that this line first shows a sharp rise, then gradually slopes more towards the horizontal, and finally rises again from the horizontal with an equally sharp curve. In other words, the average always preponderates (about 70 per cent), while the extremes at both ends form the exceptions (about 15 per cent each). Giants and dwarfs are rare, while ordinary people are in the majority. Shown diagrammatically (the number vertical, the height horizontal), one gets the following curve —which is known in mathesis as the binomium of Newton, or the curve of Gauss. (See p. 122, Diagram VI.)

Quetelet discovered this law from the chest measurement figures of Scottish recruits; later, it appeared to apply also to physical strength, eyesight, etc.—in short, to all physical qualities. At last, it became clear that we were confronted with a universal law of nature, i.e. *all individuals of the same*

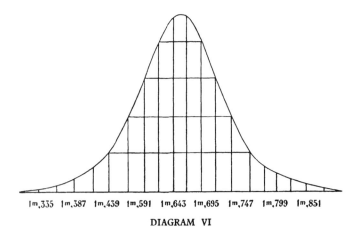

DIAGRAM VI

THE LAW OF INDIVIDUAL VARIATIONS (BODILY HEIGHT OF BELGIAN RECRUITS)
(Reprinted from Quetelet, *Physique Sociale* (II, p. 71)

species vary in their elementary qualities according to the law of Quetelet.[1]

This law also applies to the mental faculties of man. Fr. Galton, for example, has proved it for the intellect. At present there is no longer any possible doubt that this law is also universal in the spiritual world: extremes are always rare, while averages preponderate largely. And in the moral world, too, the same thing applies—very superior characters are extremely rare, and so are very inferior ones.

[1] Compare H. de Vries, *Eenheid in veranderlijkheid*, 1898 (*Unity in variability*), and his *Afstammings-en mutatieleer* (1907) (*Theory of descent and mutation*) in fine.

THE LAW OF INDIVIDUAL VARIATIONS 123

With this we have returned to the criminological field, and are now able to pose the question: what is the significance of this law for criminology? It is a curious thing that Quetelet himself has given little or no attention to this question.

In the first place—and here we come back to Ferri's formula—this law proves that we must not think of social mass-phenomena as a sort of addition sum of various individual cases. Quetelet himself uses the comparison of a large circle, which is looked at from different distances. Seen very close, it is nothing but a collection of dots; held a little farther, these dots are seen to form a line together; while, finally, the circle reveals itself as such. It may be, therefore, that the formula—a single crime = individual + environment-factors is correct for that one single case; but in the mass, this formula is wrong. If one imagines—this is the line of reasoning which Ferri and his adherents follow—the individual factor not to be there, in that particular case, then that particular crime will not be committed. Agreed! If individual A is not placed at the top, but at the bottom end of the curve, then A will not commit the crime; but, in that case, individual B will be in that place, and commit the crime instead. A very important matter indeed—for somebody who takes a particular interest in A; for sociology, however, which does not concern itself with special individuals but with society in general, it is a matter of indifference.

When one considers the problem of criminality as a mass-phenomenon—which is the way one should consider it, because that is what it is—then the law of Quetelet is also an explanation why crime, from year to year (external conditions being supposed equal) has such a regular course: the human material, with which society has to work, is fairly constant, 'Der Mensch ist ein Dauertypus', to use an anthropological phrase. There is indeed, not the remotest sign of any evidence that, as far as crime is concerned—we leave alone the question whether this is the case in any other field—selective influences have, in the course of time, wrought any change in the anthropological constitution of humanity.

In the third place, the law of individual variations teaches us that qualitative differences between human beings may also, in the last analysis, be reduced to quantitative ones. Between the giant at one end, and the dwarf at the other, there runs a long, uninterrupted sequence of gradual differences. The same is true of character: between *homo nobilis* and *homo criminalis*, too, there are countless transitory forms. This way of representing things as if the criminal—that is, of course, the serious criminal—were a species of human being quite apart, in based upon an error, which has its origin, among other things, in the ignoring of these gradations.

Fourthly, the maximum and minimum figures of the curve —assuming a sufficiently large quantity of material to be available—always lie about equally high, or, as the case may be, low. Humanity is very numerous, even when one confines oneself to the periods in which records of crime have been kept; and the material is, biologically speaking, so big that there is not much chance that the limits which are at present known to us will be exceeded in the future, neither as regards the plus, nor as regards the minus variants. Nobody would be able to imagine individuals being born with greater spiritual endowments than an Aristotle, a Shakespeare, a Rembrandt, a Beethoven, or a Goethe; and biology supports this contention on the best of grounds. Genius is a lucky combination of maximal variations in a single individual, which occurs only very rarely, as rarely for instance, as throwing eight sixes with eight dice in one throw. Mathematics teaches us that the chance of doing this with one die more—nine sixes on top—is extraordinarily much smaller. What applies to the plus-variants is, *mutatis mutandis*, also true for the minus variants. The 'plus grand des grands criminels' is an unfortunate combination of extreme variations[1] which (humanity may congratulate itself upon this fact) is equally extremely rare, and concerning which it is extremely improbable that they will come to a still lower level than that which has already

[1] Definitely not always minus variants. This, however, makes no essential difference.

THE LAW OF INDIVIDUAL VARIATIONS 125

been reached. The Landrus and the Kürtens will probably never be excelled either!

In the above we have left the 'average human being' (*l'homme moyen*) out of consideration. This was only right, as generally speaking he has little or nothing to do with crime. It would, however, be a mistake to rule him out altogether from the study of criminology. In the first place, because now and then he becomes guilty of one of the offences known as *petite criminalité*; 'anybody can get into a scrape', as the saying goes; and the Bible speaks of 'he who is without sin let him cast the first stone'. Even for this, however, it will be necessary for circumstances to be fairly unfavourable. It is also possible that environment is extraordinarily unfavourable—one need only think of a completely corrupt *milieu* during youth—in which case even the 'average man' will fall. This applies not only to the *homme moyen*, but also, sometimes, to the 'plus-variant': among criminals we sometimes find men with very good innate qualities. In such cases we speak, *in foro*, of 'victims of circumstances'. In normal times these are exceptions; in abnormal times, however, this phenomenon may grow to assume mass-proportions. During and immediately after the War-period, conditions were so extremely unfavourable that even the 'average man' began to stumble—and indeed, sometimes worse than that. If these circumstances had continued much longer this weakening of the general morale might alone have caused the downfall of civilized society.

In the above exposition it was pointed out that the general character of the curve in question does not alter. This is not to say, however, that its level is of necessity always the same. It may indeed be possible, by means of selection, to change it to some extent. If for instance, only plus-variants were allowed to reproduce themselves the general level would be raised; the average comes on a higher level, the maximum higher, and the minimum less low. Both fauna and flora have thus been improved by human interference. Eugenists imagine this to be possible also for humanity. Theoretically it must be admitted that this possibility exists. In regard to the practicability of such a measure, however, I maintain an extremely sceptical attitude. Human beings, once and for all, are not sugar-beets or cows, which can be experimented with as one pleases. We may leave out of consideration the question of the rearing of geniuses. But even the elimination of minus-variants from reproduction would entail the most tremendous difficulties; and even this would have to be done on a fairly large scale, if one wished to achieve any practical result—without even considering the fact that criminals are not all minus-variants by a long way, in the sense in which biologists understand the term; as we have seen, there is quite a lot of good human material amongst them. It cannot be denied that the eugenists have taken up a standpoint which is very remote from man and society indeed; thus, for example, they have completely ignored that other socio-pathological phenomenon, prostitution, which, owing to special circumstances, remains practically sterile—although notwithstanding this fact, it belongs just as much to the ordinary run of things in present-day society as does criminality.

However all this may be, as far as we can see into the future there seems to be no chance of any radical eugenic measures; but perhaps time will bring changes here, too. Eugenists, in the meantime, would act wisely—not all of them have as yet risen to this point of view—by making themselves familiar with the results of the researches of criminal sociology, and by co-operating in the improvement of environment, which factor, after all, dominates humanity more than predisposition does. For inborn qualities alone do not lead to crime— pathological cases excepted, of course; this has been proved beyond contradiction.

CHAPTER VII
THE SPIRITUALISTIC SCHOOL

23. GENERAL OUTLINE

QUITE a special place among the different theories in criminology is held by a school of thought which seeks the cause—or, at any rate, one of the causes—of crime elsewhere; namely, in the lack of religion. This view is usually called the spiritualistic school. To it belonged, e.g. in Germany, the previously mentioned moral-statistician A. von Oettingen (1827–1905),[1] H. Stursberg (1841–1927),[2] J. Jaeger,[3] and F. A. K. Krauss (1843–1917)[4]; in France, e.g. L. Proal (1843)[5] and H. Joly (1839–1925)[6]; in Belgium the abbé M. de Baets (1863–1931).[7] They take up quite different standpoints in regard to other causes of criminality. Some, like Stursberg and Proal, being indeterminists, deny the existence of practically any connexion between crime and society; others, like De Baets, on the contrary, place great emphasis on this connexion.

One or two quotations at random may suffice. For instance, De Baets says:

'It is in the weakening of this power' (i.e. religion), 'that I would see the chief causes of the terrifying increase in crime.'[8]

Krauss opines as follows:

'The ever-increasing estrangement from God, which is

[1] *Die Moralstatistik in ihrer Bedeutung für eine Sozialethik* (1882).
[2] *Die Zunahme der Vergehen und Verbrechen und ihre Ursachen* (1878).
[3] *Zunahme der Verbrechen und Abhilfe* (1898).
[4] *Der Kampf gegen die Verbrechensursachen* (1905).
[5] *Le crime et la peine* (1894).
[6] *Le crime* (1888).
[7] *L'école d'anthropologie criminelle* (1893), and *Les influences de la misère sur la criminalité* (1895).
[8] *Les influences*, etc., p. 19.

penetrating more and more into the wider strata of the people, and the utterly immoral views of life and the world in general which are the outcome of this, form the obscure sub-soil in which blasphemy and crime flourish exuberantly. True morality is not possible without religion.'[1]

24. CRITIQUE

When one asks what proofs are adduced in support of this bold contention, the reply must be: practically none! The only argument one meets is this: crime increases; so does irreligion—therefore: causal relation.

In the succeeding paragraphs some brief critical observations on this thesis will be made.[2] Before proceeding with these, I may remark that these authors would seem to have made a pretty free use of the above argument. Admitting that both the tendency to irreligion and that to crime point in the same direction, a connexion is thereby made feasible; but the *causal nexus* is not thereby made acceptable. They may, possibly, both be dependent upon a third factor. If one wishes to prove a definite causal relation, then it is necessary to show from another angle—i.e. the psychological—where it lies; for example, in the way it was done with the declining curves of aggressive criminality and alcoholism. The relation between crime and irreligion is not nearly so obvious as these authors seem to suppose.

Now, when we look at the figures, it appears that the course of the first series is, indeed, as was contended. In the Netherlands, for instance, the number of persons not belonging to any religious denomination increased steadily, from just over 12,000 (3 per cent) in 1879, to over 533,000 (7·7 per cent) in 1920, and to more than 1,144,000 (14·4 per cent) in 1930.

The second series, however, shows not a rise, but a fall; in 1901 the general criminality figure was 26·7 per cent per 10,000 of the population, whereas, in 1928, it amounted to

[1] o.c., p. 34.
[2] This is also done, at greater length, in my *Geloof en misdaad*, 1913 (*Religion and crime*).

its causes in the War, and was not related by any criminologist to any lack of religion. As we have pointed out before, the trend of the various kinds of crime is unmistakably connected with social events of an entirely different character—such as economic crises, alcoholism and the like.

Neither are there, as far as I can see, many historical arguments in favour of the thesis of the religious authors. In the Middle Ages atheism was unknown—but crime, on the contrary, very well known. And in England, in the beginning of the nineteenth century, we see an extraordinary increase in crime; but there is no question at all, at this time, of any widespread irreligion. Indeed, one might quite well turn the theory the other way round; when, at the end of the nineteenth and the beginning of the twentieth century, irreligion became a mass-phenomenon, crime actually decreased!

The geography of irreligion and crime in the Netherlands (as far as I am aware these figures do not exist for any other country) does not confirm the theory of De Baets and his adherents either. The southern provinces have only an insignificant proportion of non-religious persons, but criminality figures are, in those parts, far from favourable; while, on the other hand, North-Holland, Frisia, and Groningen give high percentages of non-denominational, and fairly favourable criminality figures.

The clearest illustrations can be had from criminal statistics directly—i.e. in those countries where the religious denomination of condemned persons is noted. This is the case in the Netherlands. In the following table these data are given. (See Table IX.)

Now these statistics—which cover 126,000 individual cases —teach us something quite different from the authors in question. In *all* crimes, of every description, the irreligious are at the bottom of the list! The relative figures are as follows: to every 100 non-denominational persons who are sentenced, there are 252 Israelites, 366 Protestants, and 494 Roman Catholics.

TABLE IX[1]

Persons sentenced, per 100,000 of the population, aged 10 years and over (yearly average of the years 1901–9, calculated as on December 31, 1904)

Crimes	Protestant	Roman Catholic	Jewish	No de-nomination	Total
All crimes	308·6	416·5	212·7	84·2	337·3
Simple Larceny	40·0	54·8	25·5	9·6	43·9
Aggravated larceny	19·9	24·0	12·7	5·2	20·7
Receiving stolen goods	2·6	3·5	9·2	0·7	3·0
Embezzlement	8·6	9·3	13·1	1·9	8·7
False pretences	2·4	2·5	3·9	0·4	2·4
Offences against public morals	1·9	3·4	2·0	0·5	2·4
Immoral assault	1·2	1·0	0·3	0·2	1·0
Rape, etc.	1·5	2·2	1·5	0·7	1·8
Immorality with children, etc.	0·3	0·3	0·1	0·0	0·3
All sexual offences	5·1	7·1	4·1	1·6	5·7
Assault on officials	25·9	37·0	13·2	12·2	29·0
Assault	74·4	98·2	43·2	20·1	80·1
Aggravated assault	8·5	11·0	3·9	1·9	9·1
Manslaughter and murder	0·4	0·6	0·5	0·1	0·5

[1] Reprinted from *Geloof en Misdaad*, p. 10.

TABLE X[1]

Persons sentenced, per 10,000 of the population of Amsterdam, in the years 1923–7

Offences	Protestant		Roman Catholic		Israelite		No denomination		Total	
	Male	Female	Male	Female	Male	Female	Male	Female	Male	Female
Against public order and authority	7·6	0·4	8·2	1·2	7·4	0·6	7·8	1·0	7·7	0·7
Against morals	3·2	0·6	4·6	0·7	2·9	0·3	2·0	0·9	3·2	0·6
Against life or person	8·3	1·9	8·0	2·6	9·9	2·5	6·7	2·0	8·1	2·2
Economic	23·4	2·4	28·8	3·8	23·2	0·7	14·4	1·8	22·4	2·4
Violence to property or animals	1·8	0·1	2·7	0·0	0·4	0·0	1·5	0·2	1·8	0·1
Begging and vagrancy	0·3	0·0	0·4	0·0	0·3	0·0	0·2	0·0	0·3	0·0
Other offences	0·2	0·0	0·2	0·0	0·0	0·0	0·1	0·0	0·1	0·0
Total	45·0	5·6	53·3	8·5	44·5	4·3	33·0	6·0	43·9	6·2

[1] Reprinted from *Criminaliteit in Amsterdam en van Amsterdammers* (Statistical Information, published by the Statistical Bureau of the municipality of Amsterdam, No. 94, 1932), p. 15.

132   THE SPIRITUALISTIC SCHOOL

Recently-collected data, relating to *Amsterdam* in the years 1923–7, confirm the above. The following table is derived from these figures (see Table X).

These statistics leave no loophole for misunderstanding: criminality among irreligious persons is usually the lowest on the list; only in two of the women's groups it is not favourable.[1] As I predicted in an earlier work[2] these extremely favourable figures for the non-denominational in the years 1901–9 could not possibly be maintained if irreligion steadily continued to expand. This is the case in Amsterdam, where, in 1920, more than 20 per cent of the population did not belong to any church denomination, and where at present the figure is in the neighbourhood of 34 per cent.

What the statistics teach us is confirmed by private investigation. Ferri found, among 700 murderers, one single atheist.[3] Havelock Ellis says that freethinkers are rare in prisons; he quotes the English prison clergyman J. W. Horsley, who found, among 28,351 criminals, at most 57 atheists[4]; Laurent states that irreligious persons occur among criminals 'only sometimes'[5]; Muller points out that among the professional criminals examined by him 'there were no atheists'[6]; Joly recalls that of all those who were executed in Paris in the course of thirty years, only one refused spiritual ministrations in his last moments.[7] And whoever is not yet convinced by these facts should inquire from regular visitors to the prisons in the Netherlands. He will get the same reply to his questions everywhere: irreligious criminals are met with only rarely.

This incautiously-expressed accusation, therefore, that the

---

[1] Some of the absolute figures are so low that a conclusion is hardly justified. Only four non-religious women were involved in offences of violence in five years!

[2] *Vide Geloof en misdaad*, p. 75.

[3] 'Il sentimento religioso negli omicidi' (*Archivio di psichiatria e scienzi penali*, V, 1884, p. 281).

[4] *Verbrecher und Verbrechen*, p. 173.

[5] *Les habitués des prisons de Paris*, p. 402.

[6] 'Cijfers uit de practijk' ('Figures from practice') (*Tijdschrift voor Strafrecht*, XXII, p. 463.

[7] *Le crime*, p. 237.

CRIMINALITY AMONG THE IRRELIGIOUS 133

absence of religiousness leads to crime, may herewith be considered as having been disposed of.[1]

25. THE CAUSES OF THE LOW CRIMINALITY AMONG THE IRRELIGIOUS

The above would, of course, be very incomplete, if we refrained from dealing, however briefly, with the question: what are the reasons why crime is less amongst the irreligious than amongst the religious?

The reasons are chiefly of a social nature, and have hardly anything to do with the question of 'faith or no faith'. The irreligious are, chiefly, city- and, mostly, large-city-dwellers; in 1920 their percentage in the small municipalities was 2·1, and in the large towns 15·7. They are recruited, generally, from the ranks of the intellectuals and the skilled—mostly organized workers. By virtue of their greater culture and comparatively well-to-do circumstances neither of these two groups belong to those who are susceptible to the influence of criminal ideas; and they have, moreover, more self-control.

The irreligious—that is, insofar as they hail from a religious environment—are a character-selection. To break with any tradition pre-supposes already a certain firmness; especially when this tradition is supported and protected by great instruments of power such as those at the disposal of the churches. Indeed, to their great astonishment religious people often meet among their fellow-citizens persons whose character inspires them with great respect. The Dutch ex-cabinet minister J. C. de Marez Oyens once expressed this fact, in the Dutch First Chamber, as follows: He referred to '. . . the many, who considered the Christian Revelation to be a point of view which had been abandoned, and which now amounted

[1] We need not here go into the statement, which is sometimes made, to the effect that among criminals generally there is great laxity and indifference in matters religious; there is not a vestige of evidence that this is more so in their case than among the population in general. This, however, is another problem (*Vide*, on this subject, *Geloof en misdaad*, p. 57 et seq.).

to a totally antiquated view of life, and who, nevertheless, often excelled in the very virtues which we, with our antiquated view of life, call Christian virtues—but which they prefer to call the fruits of humanitarianism'.[1]

This character-selection has, in itself, nothing to do with irreligion. In different social circumstances the picture is turned the other way about; the early Christians, for example, and the first Protestants, were certainly such a character-selection.

The fundamental error which is at the root of the theory 'irreligion leads to crime' is that without religion there cannot be any morality. Ethnology and psychology, however, tell quite a different tale. Morality has its roots in those social feelings which are peculiar to man, and even to many species of animals. Morality lies anchored more deeply in the human mind than religion does, and therefore does not rest on it. There exists, accordingly, morality without religion—as well as religion without morality.

The error in question arose through the linking up—throughout the historical period—of religion with morals, thus creating an appearance of inseparability. Moral prescriptions are not of divine, but of very earthly origin, i.e. they have in view the interests of the group within which they are in force. What we call 'Christian virtues' exist also in places where Christianity does not exist—and are exercised, very often, quite satisfactorily.[2]

What then, is the part played by religion in this connexion? It has introduced a new kind of sanction, and added to the human punishments, those of divinity, both on earth and in a hereafter. As the purpose of all punishment—including divine punishment—is inducement to acting morally, from considerations of personal interest, this divine punishment, too, has a pseudo-moral character. But genuinely moral actions have nothing whatever to do with threats of punishment and suchlike.

[1] *Handelingen* (Parliamentary Records), 1910–11, p. 325.
[2] *Vide*, e.g. my *Criminality and economic conditions*, p. 381, et seq., also *De evolutie der moraliteit* (*The Evolution of Morality*), p. 7 et seq.

CRIMINALITY AMONG THE IRRELIGIOUS 135

Finally, the question remains: is this factor, introduced from outside, of any great importance? It cannot be gainsaid that, although from the point of view of genuine morality it is merely 'Ersatz', it has been of great significance in those times when religious experience was deep and real, and this is still true for those who are truly and warmly religious. All the same, its influence has been greatly over-estimated, especially in present-day society.

In the first place, the effect of all threats of punishment is overrated. The motives which lead to crime are generally powerful, and, moreover, actively present in the human mind, whereas the fear of punishment is frequently slight, and pushed away into the subconscious. The fear of punishment belongs to 'self-interest properly understood', and must therefore be pretty strong, if it is to balance the inclination to crime. Punishment, moreover, only follows 'in case'—i.e. if the criminal is discovered and sentenced; and how many criminals do not imagine that they will manage to go scot free!

With the exception of this last point, the above also applies to punishments hereafter—and, as a matter of fact, to a greater degree even than to earthly punishment. The existence of the former has not been proved by observation, but rests on faith. This faith may have been very strong at one time; but in these sceptical times it has become very much weaker. The large masses of the people certainly do not trouble themselves permanently about this possibility; and definitely not to such an extent that the fear of it would constitute a powerful brake on criminal tendencies. And if this possibility is given any thought at all, then more often than not the person in question hopes that he will be forgiven just this once—and takes his chance.

With this last point we have arrived at the question of the influence which subjective opinion may have on objective moral dicta. Experience teaches us that this influence is very considerable. 'Life determines faith, and not vice-versa', as Paulsen once said, thus expressing one of the most fundamental truths in this field of thought. Religious people, of course, often select that aspect of their faith which suits them best, and illustrate and re-shape it according to their own nature. That is why an objective observer of religious phenomena is often inclined to conclude: there are as many religions as there are religious people! Inferior minds among the religious, as a matter of fact, know quite well how to give a neat twist to these objective prescriptions, so as to suit their purpose—and even, at times, to give such an interpretation to any downright crime they might commit, as to bring it into line with their religious professions. Times out of number an easy compromise is made by such people between their religion and their immorality.

When seen in this light the objection which one hears so often, 'after all, there are millions of religious people who are models of morality', loses its meaning entirely. Nobody, indeed, would deny the truth of this; but that is not to say that there necessarily exists any causal relation between the two. They can, of course, be quite well both religious *and* moral—although lack of self-knowledge may cause them to look at it differently. There exists no proof of the contention that strongly religious tendencies imply any strong moral predisposition. Dr. H. T. de Graaf may think that he is justified in concluding that this is, in fact, true—basing himself on the inquiry conducted by Heymans and Wiersma, and on his own investigations.[1] Speaking for myself, he has not convinced me; for that, in fact, too little is known as yet about the psychology of religion. If these inquiries and investigations had dealt with idealist tendencies in general as related to crime, the results would probably have been very much the same. It is a well-known fact that among idealists—whether religious or irreligious—there is very little crime. Havelock Ellis is of opinion that the conclusion should read the other way round: both criminals and religious people, according to him, belong to the 'emotional' type. This, I think, has not been proved either; and therefore the question remains an open one.

[1] *Geloof en misdaad* (1914).

CHAPTER VIII

ON CRIMINAL PSYCHOLOGY

CRIMINAL psychology comprises various departments: (i) the psychology of crime (theory of motives and counter-motives); (ii) the psychology of the criminal; and (iii) that of the other persons involved in the problem (e.g. witnesses). We shall be obliged to confine ourselves here to a brief survey of the history of criminal psychology, and to a few observations on the psychology of the criminal in general, and its significance for criminology.

26. THE HISTORY OF CRIMINAL PSYCHOLOGY

This history dates from the end of the 'sixties and beginning of the 'seventies of the nineteenth century. It had, however, its precursors.

(i) *The pre-history of criminal psychology.* Apart from a few observations made here and there in ancient times, and from what a few great artists—notably, Shakespeare—saw and understood intuitively, the French jurist F. G. de Pitaval (1673-1743) was the first to collect criminal-psychological material, namely, in his work *Causes célèbres et intéressantes* (1734 et seq.). After this, from 1772-88, F. Richer continued the series, while in Germany, Häring and Hitzig edited *Der Neue Pitaval* (1842-91), followed later by *Der Pitaval der Gegenwart* (1903 et seq.). We mentioned these authors previously in another connexion. As is indicated by the title, only 'interesting cases' were dealt with in this work—i.e. those which interested the reading public though generally not for scientific reasons. The only law cases dealt with were the very big ones, in which 'les plus grands des grands criminels' played a part. Until a comparatively short time ago this remained so, to the great disadvantage of criminology. About ordinary criminals—amongst whom were, of course, also many serious cases—there existed for a long time no properly reliable material.

On a higher level—more matter-of-fact and less sensationally-written—stands the publication of the previously-mentioned work by Anselm von Feuerbach (1775–1833), *Merkwürdige Kriminalrechtsfälle*, (I, 1808, II, 1811).[1] This book, however, also contained merely psychological material, and there was no question of any exhaustive treatment of the theory of the subject. It is true that at the end of the eighteenth and the beginning of the nineteenth century a large amount of literature appeared under the title of criminal psychology, but this had little in common with the subject, except the name. The most important little book is probably that of J. C. G. Schaumann (1768–1821), entitled *Ideen zu einer Kriminalpsychologie* (1792), in which, at any rate, a programme is outlined which is not entirely uninteresting.[2]

The crop is but a poor one; much more so than in other fields of criminology; and this was to remain so for a considerable time yet. The reasons for this appear to me to be mainly the following. In the first place, the poor development of psychology as an inductive science; secondly, the conception —become prominent since Pinel and Esquirol, Prichard, Morel, and others—that one should look upon the criminal as a psychopathic case; and thirdly, the coming into fashion, since Gall and Spürzheim, of the search for anthropological peculiarities in the criminal.

Owing to all this criminal psychology had got pushed into a back seat. A few authors only can be mentioned, in the years before 1870, who have paid some, if merely a passing— attention to the psychology of the criminal. Lauvergne— whom we have already mentioned—makes, in his *Les forçats*,

---

[1] A selection from these cases was published in 1913, by W. von Scholz, under the title *Merkwürdige Verbrechen in aktenmässiger Darstellung von Anselm Ritter von Feuerbach*.
[2] This survey does not lay claim to completeness. It is, however, unlikely that much more of importance will be discovered by a more thorough search.

a few interesting remarks concerning the psyche of some categories of criminals whom he had under observation. F. C. B. Avé-Lallemant (1809–92) in his *Das Deutsche Gaunerthum* (1858)—an interesting work, chiefly from a linguistic, and also, in a way, from a historical point of view—draws attention to some of the character features of the professional criminal.

(ii) *Criminal psychology between 1870 and 1900.* The founder of criminal psychology, as a practical experimental science, was the French medical man Prosper Despine (1812–92), in the second and third parts of his *Psychologie naturelle* (1868), and in his *Etude sur l'état psychique des criminels* (*Annales médico-psychologiques*, 1872). He derives his fairly extensive material from the detailed reports in *La Gazette des Tribunaux*, and similar publications. The book only deals with the *grands criminels*—but does not go in especially for *the causes célèbres*, as does De Pitaval. He groups the material according to motives, after which he traces the psychological peculiarities of the various groups.

His final conclusion is that the criminal—with the exception of some few cases—is neither physically nor mentally diseased. True, he shows certain psychic anomalies; but these do not lie in the intellect (although many criminals are only slightly, on the contrary others are extremely intelligent) but rather in the inclinations; chiefly, however, in the moral tendencies. The criminal is often driven by evil inclinations, e.g. hatred, revenge, covetousness, disinclination to work, and so on. These things are, however, not really psychic anomalies, as they occur also in quite moral sorts of people—who, however, know how to control them.

The abnormal in the criminal lies in his moral make-up. He falls short in, or misses entirely: (i) self-interest properly understood; (ii) sympathy for his fellows; (iii) moral consciousness in the narrow sense (sense of duty); he has no caution, no sympathy and no repentance. The conclusion which Despine draws from this is that the criminal[1] should

[1] N. B. Despine's investigations cover only serious criminals.

be 'educated', or, in case this has no effect, he should be 'put in a safe place'. Ordinary punishments have little or no effect.

Despine himself looks upon his own work as merely a beginning, and urges others to continue these researches in the same way. Unfortunately this excellent advice was, for the first thirty years, hardly ever acted upon.

Not long after this, as we know, the Italian school was to make its appearance on the scene, with its great emphasis on the anthropological peculiarities of the criminal. Lombroso, in the third part of his *L'uomo delinquente*, also deals with the psychology of the criminal. He does this *en passant*, giving one or two illustrations, and discussing the most divergent things, such as thieves' language, tattooing, religiosity, etc. According to him *the* criminal is unfeeling, courageous—and, yet again, cowardly—unsteady, vain, cruel, and is characterized by his tendency to indulge in wine, gaming, and women.

The other Italian authors have not achieved overmuch in this field, either. Judging by the title alone, one would expect much of Marro's *I Caratteri dei delinquenti* (1887)— but in this one will be disappointed. The work is almost entirely of an anthropological character, with only a few rather shallow psychological remarks here and there. The criminal, according to Marro, is characterized chiefly by lack of the power of reflection, and of impressionability. The most important author in the criminal-psychological field is S. Sighele, who, in his *La folla delinquente* (1892), treats of crowd-criminality

Not much else can be said of the adherents of the Italian school in other countries. Neither, for example, Aletrino's *Manual for use in the study of criminal anthropology* (1903-4), nor P. Kovalewsky (1850) in his *Psychologie criminelle* (1903) have, with their own investigations, brought the matter much further. The German biographer of Lombroso, H. Kurella, on the other hand, has, in his *Naturgeschichte des Verbrechers*, made a fairly extensive study of criminal psychology. As characteristic features of the criminal he mentions: parasitism, mendacity, lack of sense of honour, extreme sensibility to the impression of the moment, lack of pity, cruelty, vanity, and a craving for enjoyment. His indication of a possible line of future research is quite interesting.

The German critic of the Italian school *par excellence*, A. Baer, makes in his *Der Verbrecher in anthropologischer Beziehung* (1893), only a few, but very sharp observations from which his insight into the effect of environment on psychic tendencies is especially evident. According to him, the criminal constitutes an extreme case of those psychic qualities which most frequently occur in the class of people from which he hails.

In Germany, during the same period, one finds some few other works, which are entirely outside what is called the criminological schools. A. Krauss, in his *Psychologie des Verbrechens* (1884), treats chiefly of the motives of crime, but also discusses types of criminals. In 1893, H. Gross (1847–1915) publishes his famous *Handbuch für Untersuchungsrichter als System der Kriminalistik*, with, as a sequel, his further work, *Kriminal-Psychologie* (1898). It contains hardly anything about theoretical criminal psychology — e.g. the psychology of the criminal—but treats of applied criminal psychology, i.e. psychic factors, which in ascertaining and judging crimes may be called into play. The great merit of Gross, in this field, has been to be the first to originate the criticism of evidence and witnesses—which, later, was to grow into a separate branch of science.

In France, there are no criminal-psychological works of any fundamental importance to be mentioned either. *Les Archives d'anthropologie*—a journal founded by Lacassagne in 1886—which, in its sub-title, also gives an indication of 'psychologie normale et pathologique', contains, admittedly, a few psychological studies; but these form a merely subordinate part of the whole. We may mention two more authors from this period: A. Corre, *Les criminels* (1889), in which the writer gives as his opinion that the criminal is a person of a primitive psychic make-up, and E. Laurent, *Les habitués des prisons de Paris* (1890), and *Le criminel* (1908). As an ex-prison-doctor he had wide and varied opportunities for studying the material. According to his opinion the criminal is a person whose intelligence is somewhat below the average, who is improvident, has little fellow-feeling, is lazy, vain, and weak-willed.

(iii) *Criminal psychology after 1900.* Until the end of the century, criminal psychology remained the Cinderella of criminology. There are a good many works bearing the title, but containing little or nothing on the subject—this is still the position even now—while other works only contain either superficial impressions or unsystematic arrangements of not very convincing material; on the whole, *les causes célèbres* still play far too big a part. Fundamentally speaking, the labour of Despine has not yet been excelled.

With the beginning of the new century there was to be a change in this state of things. At the same time that criminal anthropology recedes to the background criminal psychology begins to come into its own: its investigations grow more frequent and extensive, and rise to a higher level.

It was *Austria* and *Germany* which were the leading countries in this new movement. One of the great merits of H. Gross was the founding, in 1898, of the *Archiv für Kriminalanthropologie und Kriminalistik* (for short: *Gross 'Archiv*)[1], of which more than ninety volumes have already appeared. It is, in the words of our easterly neighbours, 'eine richtige Fundgrube' ('a real treasure-trove') for the whole science of criminology, especially for criminalistics; but also, in many ways, for criminal psychology. Excellent indices facilitate the finding of the relevant material.

In 1904, Aschaffenburg follows, with his *Monatschrift für Kriminalpsychologie und Strafrechtsreform*, which also contains a lot of material as well as separate studies, while an index for the first sixteen yearly volumes has also appeared. A short

[1] In 1916 (commencing with vol. 66) the title was changed to *Archiv für Kriminologie*. The present editor is Dr. R. Heindl. It is at present devoted chiefly to the study of criminalistics.

time previously, in 1903, this author had published his well-known *Das Verbrechen und seine Bekämpfung*, with, as subtitle, *Einleitung in die Kriminal-Psychologie*. About the psychology of the criminal, however, this long and detailed work contains only a few pages. The author states as his opinion that for some time to come we shall not be able to write the psychology of *the* criminal. For that, the whole image is, as yet, too kaleidoscopic, and too exclusively drawn from the very rarest and most exceptional cases. The vast majority of ordinary cases should first be arranged, according to category, and then examined. There is one single particular—the most easily measurable—which, according to him, should be mentioned, i.e. backwardness of intellectual powers. On closer examination of the various categories no doubt others will appear.

'One thing, however, I consider altogether unlikely, i.e. that we shall ever be able to isolate these peculiarities so unmistakably that we are justified in identifying them with especially criminal proclivities; they will never be anything more to us than landmarks of a definite tendency in a certain direction.'[1]

The works which appeared during the following years did not bring the matter much further. Sommer's *Kriminalpsychologie und strafrechtliche Psychopathologie* (1904) contains practically nothing about psychology. P. Pollitz's little —and, on the whole, interesting book, *Die Psychologie des Verbrechers* (*Kriminalpsychologie*) (1909) contains only some character-drawings of the professional criminal. In 1908 there appears E. Wulffen's grandly-conceived *Psychologie des Verbrechers*[2] (two volumes, about 1,000 pp. in all)—the contents of which deal, for the greater part, with other matters. The greater part of the material dealing with the psychology of the criminal is mere compilation-work. The treatment only gets

[1] p. 209, 3rd edition (1923).
[2] In 1926, under another title, i.e. *Kriminal-psychologie*.

interesting in those places where the writer recounts something from his own wide experience. His conclusion is:

'I was principally concerned to show that the psychic states and urges of the transgressor of the law are merely "playful" forms of "normal" psychic activities, from which they often deviate only very slightly, always gradually, and never without intermediary stages.'[1]

Shortly after, M. Kaufmann publishes *Die Psychologie des Verbrechens* (1912), which is theoretically rather confused, but which is based upon a wide experience of his own, and contains much important material concerning ordinary criminals, and also concerning prostitutes.

In 1912, under the leadership of K. von Lilienthal, F. Nissl, S. Schott, and K. Wilmanns, the so-called *Heidelberger Abhandlungen* ('Abhandlungen aus dem Gesamtgebiete der Kriminalpsychologie') begin to appear. In the Introduction it is pointed out that our knowledge of very special crimes and criminals is not really of much use to us.

'It is not the knowledge of unusual and mysterious crimes which forms the foundation for the understanding of the causes of, and for the practical and effectual prevention and fight against, criminality, but the systematic and unprejudiced investigation into the cases of persons detained in our penal institutions.'[2]

The first publication of this series is that by H. W. Gruhle, *Die Ursachen der jugendlichen Verwahrlosung und Kriminalität* (1912), an excellent work, which deals chiefly with other problems, but which, nevertheless, has a psychological significance.

In 1913, the same author, together with A. Wetzel, commences a fresh series, parallel to this, entitled *Verbrechertypen* —also with the exclusive intention of producing good psychological material.

[1] *Kriminalpsychologie*, p. 8.   [2] *Zur Einführung*, p. 111.

'This series aims, not at selecting the cases according to their remarkable and extraordinary features; on the contrary, it will endeavour to paint the *average criminal* in detail.'[1]

The first publication *Geliebtenmörder* (1913), is from the pen of A. Wetzel and K. Wilmanns; the second, *Säufer als Brandstifter* (1914), by H. W. Gruhle, K. Wilmanns, and G. L. Dreyfus; the third, *Zur Psychologie des Massenmordes* (1914), by R. Gaupp. From the titles of these works it is evident that the authors' original intention to confine themselves to a description of the *average criminal*, was not adhered to. Evidently, to do so entails peculiar difficulties; and the thought naturally occurs to one (time and again one comes to this conclusion) that the psychology of this average criminal does not differ so greatly from that of the non-criminal person, as to render possible, or even justify, any special description.

The War, as well as post-war conditions, interrupted these publications; they are now, however, being resumed. Apart from various monographs, we may finally mention: for Germany, M. H. Göring, *Kriminalpsychologie* (a sub-section of G. Kafka's *Handbuch der vergleichenden Psychologie*, 1922), a not very important publication which, however, gives a very extensive bibliography (more than 500 items).

The Netherlands. In 1906, *Bijdragen tot de psychologie van den misdadiger* (*Contributions to the study of the Psychology of the Criminal*) appear, from the pen of J. V. van Dijck (1878–1930), later Professor of criminal law at the university of Amsterdam. In a strictly scientific manner he has determined certain classes of *grands criminels*, according to the biographical method (factual material being derived from the *Neue Pitaval*, and similar works), and allotted them their respective places in the 'temperament' scheme of Heymans, finally adding some remarks on the psychology of the criminal in general. The material is of a very special nature—it hails from all sorts of countries and different periods, and only deals with the very worst of cases—so that the conclusions

[1] *Zur Einführung*, p. 5.

concerning *the* criminal, especially as comparative facts among the non-criminal population are lacking, are not too reliable. Apart from this, however, it is one of the best, if not the best criminal psychological work published up to that time, and it is very much to be regretted that there exists no publication of it in any of the world-languages.

Another two meritorious works by pupils of Heÿmans should be mentioned: W. A. Pannenborg's *Bijdrage tot de psychologie van den misdadiger, in 't bijzonder van den brandstichter* (1912) (*Contribution to the psychology of the criminal, more especially the incendiary*), and Dr. H. T. de Graaf (1875–1930) *Karakter en behandeling van veroordeelden wegens landlooperij en bedelarij* (1914) (*Character and treatment of persons sentenced for vagrancy and begging*).

In the meantime, another Dutch criminologist, Dr. A. N. Muller, had been working along other lines, in his *Biografisch-aetiologisch onderzoek over recidive bij misdadigers tegen den eigendom* (1908) (*Biographical-etiological inquiry into recidivism among criminals against property*). Keeping quite outside all academic psychological views he has, on the basis of a study of criminal records and personal investigation, given a very interesting psychological portrait of the professional criminal and proved thereby that along this road, too, much may be achieved.

United States of North America. Up to about 1910, the United States of America could not show any important work of their own. The International Penitentiary Congress, however, which was held at Washington in that year, resulted in the founding of the 'American Institute for Criminal law and criminology', which caused certain European works, among which were also some of a psychological character, to be translated, and which decided to start the publication of the *Journal of Criminal Law and Criminology* (1910), in which a number of psychological studies appeared serially.

Among the American criminal-psychological books the most important are: W. Healy, *The Individual Delinquent* (1915), which comprises a lot of material, and is, at the same time,

THE PSYCHOLOGY IN GENERAL 147

a manual for investigation; W. T. Root, Jr., *A psychological and educational survey of* 1916 *prisoners in the Western Penitentiary of Pennsylvania* (1926), and C. Murchison, *Criminal Intelligence* (1926), in which, by comparative study of criminals and non-criminals, with the aid of the co-called 'army-tests', an end was made, once and for all, of the often-expressed opinion that *the* criminal was chiefly characterized by very poor intellectual gifts.

England. We previously remarked that in England much practical, but on the other hand, little theoretical criminological work had been done. In 1914, Ch. Goring made up the leeway by publishing his earlier-mentioned famous book *The English Convict*, which was chiefly devoted to attacking the anthropological theories of Lombroso; it contains, however, also a chapter on the psychology of the criminal.

After the war, an enhanced interest began to be taken in the subject in England also. We may mention B. Hollander, *The psychology of misconduct, vice, and crime* (1922), M. Hamblin Smith, *The psychology of the criminal* (1923), a book with a psycho-analytical trend, C. Burt's splendid book *The Young Delinquent* (1925), and G. W. Pailthorpe's *What we put in prison* (1932).

27. THE PSYCHOLOGY OF THE CRIMINAL IN GENERAL

It will be clear from the above that the great failing which, in the beginning, marred the science of criminal psychology was the gross generalization. *The* criminal is cruel, vain, sensual, etc., etc.

The collection of material which we now have at our disposal, and the way in which it has been sifted and arranged permits us to tackle the matter differently. We should, first of all, form sharply-defined groups of crimes; after that, we should trace the peculiar psychic qualities which are character-features of the persons who committed the different crimes; only then can we attempt to find out what might be characteristic of *the* criminal.

The author of the present book has reached the conclusion, on the grounds of literature at his disposal—frequently found spread about various periodicals—that there are at least twenty-five well-defined groups of criminals: in each of which, moreover, numerous shadings may be observed. Some of these groups are well known, others fairly well, while others again are still waiting for their analysers to describe them. The differences between the various groups as such are very great; so that it is extremely difficult, if not downright impossible, to get a clear idea of what it is that characterizes *the* criminal. A few instances, taken from those groups about which ample literature is available, while an adequate degree of concordance exists, concerning the type among the various authors, may suffice to make this clear.

The tramp is characterized—this is the general opinion—by nothing so much as by his lack of activity; which as a matter of fact, is a quality which occurs fairly frequently in other economic offenders also. Now, nothing would be more foolish than to stamp this as a general feature of *the* criminal. Among the sexual, and chiefly among the aggressive transgressors of the law, this type is not found especially frequently.

The sexual criminal has, as the most obvious quality (indeed, how could it be otherwise, one might ask) an intense sensuality; and this occurs also in some categories of the economic criminal (professional). But nothing could be more unreasonable than to say: *the* criminal is abnormally sensual. Several of the groups do not show anything extraordinary in this respect.

There are, among economic criminals, some groups in which a pronounced craving for luxury is very prominent. It is, however, a glaring error to suppose that *the* criminal is always characterized by such tendencies.

More than once—especially in Holland—it has been stated that *the* criminal is a person in whom the 'primary function' is prominently developed. True, this type of person occurs fairly frequently among criminals—just as it does, in fact, among non-criminals. But it is also a fact, that, among the very gravest of offenders, it is the type whose secondary function is strongly pronounced (the demonic type), which occurs most frequently. The primary function, of course, does not pre-dispose to great actions; neither for good nor for evil.

How often one hears it stated that *the* criminal is unintelligent. There is some truth in this—as regards some of the groups, that is—e.g. for some of the sexual criminals. As against that, we see that others—e.g. the professional criminal—actually excel in intelligence.

In this way, one might continue this list for a long time. We find, among criminals, all possible human types, without being able to say with certainty that the frequency of their occurrence differs to any important extent from that among the rest of the population. It did strike me, however, that the phlegmatic type (non-emotional, active, strong secondary functions) is not one of great frequency among criminals. Which is not to say, of course, that it is more frequent among other people.

If one asks: what is *the* psychological type of the criminal, then I believe the answer must be that it does not exist. To the further question, whether, in that case, there is not a single particular which, speaking very generally, characterizes *the* criminal as such, I would reply: if anything, his moral weakness. Biologically speaking, he is a moral minus-variant. Next to this, one may suppose him to have grossly materialist inclinations. In this connexion, I would draw attention to the keen insight of Prosper Despine, who, more than sixty years ago, came to the same conclusion, although based on comparatively small factual material.

28. THE SIGNIFICANCE TO CRIMINOLOGY OF THE PSYCHOLOGY OF THE CRIMINAL[1]

The practical significance of the psychology of the criminal is beyond any doubt whatever. It has its utility for every kind

[1] Lack of space has prevented the psychology of witnesses' evidence and of confession from being treated of in the preceding paragraphs.

of practitioner of penal law. This is, of course, not to say that intelligent practitioners cannot acquire a large amount of knowledge in this field, through experience in the course of their practice; but this experience is usually bought dearly, because of the many errors which, naturally, are made in the beginning. It is therefore better to profit by systematically-recorded experiences of others, which can afterwards be supplemented with one's own observations.

Detective officers find it useful to know what psychological types run the greatest risk of committing a given kind of crime; while for members of the Public Prosecution Department and judges, it is important to know the measure of danger to public safety which inheres in certain types, for the fixing of the punishment to be asked for, the punishment to be inflicted, or the correctional measures to be taken. Much too much attention is still being given to the offence instead of to the offender. To mention only a few instances: the very rare cases of so-called 'family murder' in *foro* are, as far as punishment is concerned, considered as on a par with e.g. murder and robbery; whereas the poor wretches who go in for this sort of thing want to commit suicide, and in their distraction (from altruistic notives, if you please!) resort to this crime. Their murder really amounts to indirect suicide. Neither special prevention—there is no danger whatever of recurrence—nor general prevention justify action of such extreme severity. Persons who commit what is called non-intentional offences are usually considered as not very dangerous, according to an old dogma, which also finds expression (in the penal codes) in the fixed light punishments. This is, psychologically speaking, not entirely correct. There are amongst these offenders frequently very dangerous individuals —such as, for instance, the speed maniacs—to whom the death or maiming of their victims is a matter of complete indifference, and with whom recurrence is very probable.

It needs perhaps no stress that a knowledge of these is indispensable in criminal procedure. In this connexion we must point to the great desirability of elementary forensic psychiatrics not being *terra incognita* to the judiciary.

Notwithstanding this, they are often punished only lightly by the judge, whereas to tackle them firmly once, might conceivably cause them to refrain from repeating the offence.

In former times, when the judge had only one single kind of punishment at his disposal, and could only vary the dose, a knowledge of character was not so imperative as it is to-day, when so many courses are open to him. For the selection of the right type of punishment or corrective measure it is necessary to have some knowledge, for instance of the sensitiveness to the pain inflicted by the punishment, and to weigh the relative importance of the primary and secondary functions (the latter being important in the case of sentences on remand, and for the conditions to be imposed in those cases), and the susceptibility to educative influences of the particular type to which the offender in question belongs.

Finally, a knowledge of criminal psychology is especially useful to all those whose task is the putting into execution of punishments which deprive the individual of his liberty. The way to tackle a detained person with any chance of success partly depends on this. To treat all kinds of characters in the same way—for example with severity—will lead to results quite opposite to those intended.

On the other hand the importance of the psychology of the criminal for *criminal etiology* cannot, in my opinion, be rated highly. It has been the means of proving that certain types of human beings are more readily disposed to committing various sorts of offences than others. This does not prevent the same types from occurring also amongst ordinary people, in other words, one is not justified in calling their qualities especially criminal ones. Whether or not a person with such a psychical disposition actually becomes a criminal depends on other factors. Thus, for example, a ready-tongued, imaginative, epicurean sanguinist is certainly more gifted for obtaining money by false pretences than a monosyllabic, sober-minded phlegmatic with few material needs; but it would be quite as improper as it would be mistaken—not to say dangerous—to say to the former: 'you are pre-destined to become a swindler'. A person with a strong sexual urge is more in danger of committing some offence in that direction than anybody with weak inclinations; but the number of the former is legion, and the majority never think of acting criminally.

In the etiology of crime the psychological factor is the constant, and the environment the variable. In accordance with scientific terminology the variable is called the cause. In the same way one speaks of an unhygienic environment— e.g. polluted drinking water—as 'the cause' of infectious diseases such as cholera; although in that case, too, predisposition is not the same in every person.

CHAPTER IX

CRIMINOLOGY AS AN APPLIED SCIENCE

CRIMINOLOGY as an applied science—about which only a few remarks can be made to finish this little work—consists, just like medical science, of two parts: the prophylaxis of crime (criminal hygiene), and the treatment of criminals (criminal policy).

29. CRIMINAL HYGIENE

'Prevention is better than cure'—this, an old maxim of medical science—has been put into practice more and more generally since the middle of the nineteenth century, when scientifically-founded hygiene was introduced, and became its most important component. The greatest medical triumphs (e.g. the enormous reduction in mortality) humanity owes largely to the science of hygiene.

The same applies to criminology. It is better to prevent crime than to attempt to induce the criminal to return to the right path. 'Better' also means, in this connexion, simpler, more practical, and cheaper. What the old proverb says of illnesses: 'they come on horseback, and go on foot', is true here, too.

We have previously seen that criminal sociology shows the roads along which prophylaxis should go; and perhaps eugenics will, in the future, have a certain—be it a secondary—part to play in this respect. However important the criminal problem may be for society, yet it would amount to overestimation to imagine that, up to the present, criminological points of view have been taken into serious consideration, let alone been decisive, when measures of a social character were taken. It is possible that in the future this will be the case to a greater extent; but even so, this will at best have a secondary importance.

When dealing previously with the course of criminality

during the last half-century, I pointed out that the greatest social event of that period, i.e. the raising of the fourth estate, was a favourable factor in that course. It is here that the central point of the whole problem lies. To make prosperity and culture as general as possible is the best preventive against crime; prosperity, we said, not luxury. There is not a weaker spot to be found in the social development of our times than the present ever-growing and ever-intensifying covetousness, which, in its turn, is the result of powerful social forces. As long as this development is not interrupted the crimes which are bound up with it will increase rather than decrease. Everything which tends to further a healthy family life, and therefore acts for the good of the child; the care of neglected children, good education, development of the spiritual powers slumbering in the people—and, no less, of the physical ones— all this points in this direction. The fundamental problem in all this is to what extent social development can be made to further the development of the moral powers of man. In this respect a certain—if moderate—optimism is permissible. The moral isolation in which the nineteenth century placed man is being broken through; and the social side of his nature is beginning to come to the fore. This optimism can only be expressed in moderate terms, however; for the struggle between various groups has taken possession of the people's mentality more violently than ever before, and the light of general social consciousness can be seen but faintly at the horizon.

As against the theory of the 'born criminal', that of 'environment' justifies us in taking heart and displaying activity. We need not let our heads hang—on the contrary, we must work as energetically as never before, for results are assured. As long as humanity remains so far away from its (provisionary) ideal—the ensuring of a fairly decent existence for every one of its members—it is idle to dispute about the question: will there ever come a time when there will be no more crime? As individual occurrence, crime will of course always exist; if only because there will always be mentally-diseased people, whose conduct cannot be in accordance with any social order.

CRIMINAL HYGIENE 155

For crime as a mass-phenomenon, however, it is quite feasible that it should disappear. Certain types of crime have in fact disappeared, together with the social soil in which they throve; and one can also point to certain groups of the population in present-day society, whose living conditions are such as to render mass-crime unknown there. It is, however, far from the thoughts of the author to start an argument about this aspect of the matter. Personal temperament plays its part and a very important one it is in these matters. We may, however, remind pessimists that even Aristotle was of opinion that slavery would exist eternally, as it was part of human nature; while optimists should not forget that the law of individual differences will always continue in force. Humanity will always count bad variants among its numbers, and even should they not all become criminals they will still remain a long way from the *homo nobilis*. In this respect, too, trees won't grow up into the sky!

30. CRIMINAL POLICY

There finally remains the question: what does criminology —chiefly, of course, psychology, but also sociology—teach us concerning the treatment of the criminal?

Punishment has its origin in revenge; but besides this, it has also served (in the beginning quite unconsciously) to protect society (*la défense sociale*) against dangerous individuals. This last element has, in the course of time—especially latterly—grown stronger and more conscious; and the element of revenge is beginning to lose more and more ground. It is my firm conviction that the principle of revenge is destined to disappear completely from all criminal law. A day will come when penal law will be cleansed of every thought of punitive compensation; and when the community will be able, with a clean conscience, to say to the criminal: 'I have also your own interest at heart!' No longer shall we regard the past, but we shall look into the future; 'correctional' punishment is sure to prevail in the end. We should not, however, cherish any illusions concerning the period when this will happen, for the feeling of revenge lies deep in the heart of man.

What should, according to criminology, be done about the criminal?[1] A programme of action has gradually taken shape, in its main parts, as the science developed; fortunately, a not unimportant part of it is no longer a mere programme as a commencement has been made with putting it into practice. Child law has shown the way; and has even, in many cases, realized a good bit of it.

The first demand of criminology is that the criminal's mental health should be examined; and if this is shown to be disturbed, treatment should follow accordingly. Although, of course, punishment is not excluded in such cases, the rule should be that medical treatment is indicated, under judicial guarantee, of course, that the safety of the community remains assured.

The first thing to ascertain for criminals who are sound in mind, is whether or not restriction of their personal liberty is absolutely necessary. If this is not the case, a fine will generally be the punishment indicated. Providing it be suitable to the financial circumstances of the offender, and collected by a suitable method of payment, it has been proved to be a very effectual punishment. In certain cases, even a conditional fine may have its uses.

In cases where a mere fine is not sufficient, a threat of restriction of liberty (conditional sentence; when accompanied by special conditions, this amounts really to treatment of criminals in free society[2]) is indicated. This was first introduced nearly half a century ago. It was later applied universally, and has proved a great success. The conditional sentence has been a great lesson to those who saw the only remedy in severity of punishment as well as to those who

---

[1] The majority of petty offenders are not, of course, to be considered here, a money fine being in their case the punishment indicated.

[2] In certain cases, a fine, combined with a conditional sentence, may not be misplaced; sometimes also partly conditional, partly unconditional restriction of liberty.

thought that the mere threat of punishment was not an efficient brake on criminality. The imposition of fines and conditional sentences tends to effect a considerable reduction in the number of short-term imprisonments. These then remain in reserve for those cases in which a good effect may be expected from a sharp correction; i.e. cases in which little or nothing can be expected from educative measures, and which, accordingly, demand cellular imprisonment.

There remain the more serious cases. Here, the first thing to ascertain is whether any good result may be achieved by 'forced', i.e. reformatory, education. In the case of children, this is always imperative; with young persons[1] very often, and in cases of young adults frequently advisable; the thing is, in these matters, not to despair too soon. Numerous criminals are neglected individuals, who, after all, should have one good chance of learning how to adapt themselves to the demands of society. The results in those countries where this reformatory education exists, are encouraging.

In cases where the idea of interfering by means of reformatory education is misplaced, ordinary detention should ensue. The difficulty of fixing the duration for this is considerable, and will always remain so. Any fixed length of time for it will always be more or less arbitrary. A correction of this has been found in the form of the 'conditional discharge' (on parole) which ends the detention when it is no longer thought necessary in view of the safety of the community.

The method to be used in applying detentionary punishments form one of the most tricky problems with which practical criminology is faced. Punishment of criminals in a body, without selection and education, has proved in practice to be a great mistake—it has indeed, not without good reason, been called 'the criminal university'. The reaction to this— cellular imprisonment—has proved an error only slightly less serious. Weakened both physically and mentally,

[1] It is here immaterial whether it should be the civil courts or otherwise, to which cases of this kind ought to be referred; also whether one should speak, not of 'punishments' but of 'corrective measures'.

unaccustomed to ordinary work, which in present-day society is hardly ever done alone by anybody, unaccustomed also to human intercourse, the discharged man leaves the prison, more poorly equipped than ever for the struggle for existence. The solution is probably to be found in a combination of what is suitable in both these systems: a limited and selected community, and isolation during the night. This method will also provide opportunities for the application—be it in a limited form—of the educative idea, which always has its value.[1] Doctors do not talk straightaway of 'incurable' patients either; and it would be a good thing if their example were followed in the field of criminal law. Working in a well-appointed factory, or on the land, more closely resembles ordinary life in freedom, and offers a better chance of success after discharge, than cellular labour does. For those who feel, or prove to be, unfit for communal life, the cell remains the place indicated during meals and recreation time.

There remain, now, the very gravest of cases: the *grands criminels*; the professional and habitual criminals. For these people, long-term detention (called in England 'preventive detention') is imperative,[2] however much mitigated one may imagine the *régime* to be. An unjust reproach is frequently levelled at modern criminology, namely that it has wanted to be too soft in dealing with the criminal. This reproach should be returned to whence it came: the classic school has been too severe towards ordinary criminals, for they are often more troublesome than dangerous, and too soft with the really dangerous individuals, especially with professional criminals. In some cases, of course, we have to be severe, but only when experience shows that it is necessary. Sometimes, too, the judge is not in a position to leave out of consideration entirely

---

[1] It goes without saying that a prison staff which is equal to this extremely heavy task, is necessary.

[2] I do not feel called upon to discuss the death penalty which, in my opinion, is a barbaric relic of former times. In the Netherlands it was abolished in 1870: the last execution took place in 1861. Criminality-figures in this country are low and the crimes are not generally of a grave nature.

the thought of general prevention, and is obliged to act more severely than the case which has been submitted to him would, in itself, have necessitated. Whoever might stamp this as a reactionary view does not know the psychology of some classes of criminals, nor realize the dangers which threaten society from that quarter. The final consideration in all this, however, should never be the desire for revenge, but, solely, social necessity. Severity—which is sometimes necessary—and humanity are not mutually inconsistent or exclusive. Doctors, too—I may be permitted one more comparison with their profession—are not infrequently obliged to interfere drastically, and not spare the patient a certain amount of pain in order to prevent worse.

The same applies to criminal law. Providing always, that one deeply realizes the tragedy which is part of the nature of crime; providing, also, that one keeps clearly before one's mind's eye the fact that criminals are among the most unhappy of our fellow-beings, and that, therefore, it is our duty to exercise the greatest humanity in our treatment of them. *Le vice aussi est une misère. . . .*

APPENDIX I
LIST OF CRIMINOLOGICAL CONGRESSES, SOCIETIES AND PERIODICALS[1]

A. CONGRESSES

1. Since 1872 (London), *International Penitentiary Congresses* are held, at intervals of about five years, by what was later called the International Penitentiary Commission. They have been held at Stockholm (1878), Rome (1885), St. Petersburg (1890), Paris (1895), Brussels (1900), Budapest (1905), Washington (1910), London (1925), Prague (1930), and Berlin (1935).

The first of these congresses were attended chiefly by prison officials in order to discuss penitentiary questions, in the restricted sense of the word; but at the later ones other penal law subjects have increasingly been discussed—such as, for example, the conditional and the indefinite sentence; and one is therefore justified in saying that at these congresses applied criminology in the widest sense is dealt with. Since 1930 (Prague) the name is 'Congrès Pénal et Pénitentiaire International'. The lengthy and detailed *Actes* are indispensable for the knowledge and history of practical criminology.

2. Since 1885, *International Congresses for Criminal anthropology* (*biology and sociology*) have been held. They are the following: Rome (1885), Paris (1889), Brussels (1892), Genève (1896), Amsterdam (1901), Turin (1906), Cologne (1911). The next one should have been held in Budapest in 1915, but dropped out owing to the war. Since then they have not been resumed, there being no international organization in existence for their convocation. Their aims are purely theoretical. The *Actes* (sometimes called *Compte(s) Rendu(s)*, or *Berichte*) are also indispensable for the knowledge of theoretical criminology.

B. SOCIETIES
a. International

1. The oldest in existence is the *Commission Pénitentiaire*

[1] This list makes no claim to completeness. The author will be indebted for any additions and/or corrections.

162   APPENDIX I

Internationale (at present *Commission Pénale et Pénitentiaire Internationale*), founded in 1872, at the instigation of the United States of America, and comprising the governments of practically all civilized countries. Its chief task is the organization of the congresses mentioned sub. A 1, and the publication of the *Actes*. The Commission also publishes a *Bulletin* from time to time. Since 1926 it has its own permanent office at Bern, under direction of its Secretary-General, Professor Dr. J. Simon van der Aa, formerly professor of criminal law at Groningen.

2. In 1889 the *Union Internationale de Droit Pénal* (*Internationaler Kriminalistischer Verein*) was founded on a modern criminological footing by Professors van Hamel, Von Liszt, and Prins. It has held regular meetings and published a *Bulletin* printed in French and German. Owing to the war it fell apart as an international society. The German section of this society maintained its existence as an independent body. Latin students of criminal law ignore its existence.

3. The latter therefore founded, in 1924, at Paris, the *Association Internationale de Droit Pénal*. The countries which have joined this organization are: France, Belgium, Italy, Spain, Roumania, Poland, and the United States of America. It does not take up a modern standpoint. 'Elle ne prend pas parti entre les diverses écoles de criminalistes'. Its organ is *Revue internationale de droit pénal* (1924) and its secretary Professor J. A. Roux (Paris).

b. National

To these belong, in the first place, the sections of the international societies mentioned above, sub. 2 and 3. Neither England nor the Netherlands, however, have formed any national sections.

THE NETHERLANDS

1. In 1907 Professors van Hamel, Simons, and Winkler founded the *Psychiatrisch-Juridisch Gezelschap*. As is evident from the title, this is not a general criminological society, but the subjects dealt with at its meetings were not kept strictly within its limited scope. Its reports are of considerable importance for criminology in the Netherlands. During the

APPENDIX I   163

last few years the society has extended its borders, and now also admits interested non-alienists and non-jurists as members, while it also has extended somewhat the field of its activities. The secretary is Dr. S. P. Tammenoms Bakker (Amsterdam).

2. The *Nederlandsche Vereeniging voor Geestelijke Volksgezondheid* (*Vereeniging voor Psychische Hygiene*), founded in 1930, comprises in its field of study also criminality. Reports of its meetings are published. The secretary is Dr. F. S. Meyers (Amsterdam).

3. The *Nederlandsch Genootschap tot Zedelijke Verbetering der Gevangenen* (1822) is the oldest society in existence, dealing practically and theoretically with penitentiary questions. Although it has retained its old (and antiquated) name it has moved along with the times, and still remains the leading organization in this field. Its organ is *Maandblad voor berechting en reclasseering van volwassenen en kinderen* (1922). Its secretary is Dr. N. Muller (Amsterdam).

4. *De Vereeniging voor Strafrechtspraak* (1923). Until 1927 his society was called *Vereeniging voor Kinder-en Politierechtspraak*.

5. *Nederlandsche Bond voor Strafrecht* (1932).

UNITED STATES OF AMERICA

The leading society is the *American Institute of criminal law and criminology* (1910), situated at Chicago; secretary Newman F. Baker. Organ: *Journal of criminal law and criminology* (1910).

One of the best-known older organizations is the *American Prison Association* (1870). The *National Committee for Mental Hygiene* (1909), situated at New York, also occupies itself with the study of the problem of criminality. Organs: *Mental Hygiene* (quarterly) (1922), and *Mental Hygiene Bulletin* (monthly) (1928).

GREAT BRITAIN

The most important organization is the *Howard League for Penal Reform* (1921), situated at London; secretary Miss C. M. Craven. This society originated in a fusion between the

Howard Association (1866) and the *Penal Reform League* (1907). Organ: *The Howard Journal* (1930).
Institute for the scientific treatment of delinquency (1933).

FRANCE

Société Générale des Prisons (1877), situated in Paris. Organ: *Revue Pénitentiaire et de droit pénal* (1877). Since 1931 (Vol. 55) the words *et études criminologiques* have been added to its title.

C. PERIODICALS

THE NETHERLANDS

1. *Tijdschrift voor Strafrecht* (1886). Founded and edited by the Dutch professors of criminal law. From time to time criminological subjects are also dealt with.[1] Very extensive bibliography (also on criminology).
2. *Maandblad voor berechting en reclasseering van volwassenen en kinderen* (1922). Editor: Dr. N. Muller.
3. *Mensch en Maatschappij* (1925).[2] Intended for the treatment of various anthropological, sociological, and psychological subjects, among which also criminology. Secretary-editor, Professor H. N. ter Veen.

GREAT BRITAIN

1. *The Sociological Review* (1908). Editors: A. M. Carr-Saunders, A. Farquharson, and M. Ginsberg.
2. *The Medico-legal and Criminological Review* (1933). Editors: G. Scot and E. Dickson.

UNITED STATES OF AMERICA

1. *Journal of Criminal Law and Criminology* (1910) appears

[1] Publications other than the Dutch ones, of a purely criminal law character, also discuss, of course, subjects of a criminological nature from time to time. Only a few are mentioned here.
[2] In other countries anthropological, sociological, and psychological periodicals also contain, of course, criminological subjects from time to time. They are not mentioned here.

at Chicago, under editorship of Professor Robert H. Gault.
2. *Mental Hygiene* (1922).
3. *Mental Hygiene Bulletin* (1928).

BELGIUM

1. *Revue de droit pénal et de criminologie* (1907), founded by R. de Rijckère and H. Jaspar. Edited by J. Gillard.
2. *L'Ecrou*. Organe de la Fédération des fonctionnaires et des employés des prisons (1920).

GERMANY

1. *Zeitschrift für die gesammte Strafrechtswissenschaft* (1879), founded by F. von Liszt, and now under the editorship of—among others—Professor E. Kohlrausch (Berlin). Contains from time to time—especially so in the first years of its publication—also criminological contributions.
2. *Archiv für Kriminalanthropologie und Kriminalistik* (1898) founded by the Austrian H. Gross. It has now got into German hands, and is edited by Dr. R. Heindl. Since 1916 (Vol. 66) its name is *Archiv für Kriminologie*, and it is at present chiefly devoted to criminalistics.
3. *Monatschrift für Kriminalpsychologie und Strafrechtsreform* (1904), founded by Professor G. Aschaffenburg, and now under the editorship of—among others—Professor F. Exner. Stopped publication during the War, but appearing again since then.
4. *Blätter für Gefängniskunde* (1864). Zeitschrift des Vereins der deutschen Strafanstaltsbeamten.

FRANCE

1. *Revue pénitentiaire et de droit pénal et Etudes criminologiques* (1877).
2. *Archives d'anthropologie criminelle, de criminologie et de psychologie normale et pathologique* (1886), founded by A. Lacassagne and G. Tarde. Was for a long time one of the best criminological journals. Stopped publication in 1914.
3. *Etudes criminologiques* (1926). Organ of 'L'association

des élèves et anciens élèves de l'Institut de Criminologie de l'Université de Paris'. Editor: M. Gabriel El Banna. Ceased to exist in 1930.

ITALY

1. *Archivio di psichiatria, anthropologia criminale e scienze penali* (1880), founded by C. Lombroso. The present name is *Archivio di anthropologia criminale e medicina legala*.
2. *La Scuola Positiva* (1891), founded by E. Ferri.
3. *Rivista di Diritto Penitenziario*. Studi teoretici e pratici. Editor: G. Novelli.

SWITZERLAND

Schweizerisches Zeitschrift für Strafrecht ('Revue Pénale Suisse'), founded in 1889 by Professors C. Stooss and E. Zürcher. At present under the editorship of Professor E. Delaquis (Geneva) and others.

APPENDIX II

CRIMINOLOGICAL LITERATURE[1]

A. WORKS OF A GENERAL CHARACTER

G. Aschaffenburg, *Das Verbrechen und seine Bekämpfung*, 3rd ed., 1923.
B. Brasol, *The Elements of Crime*. 1927.
A. Elster and H. Lingemann, *Handwörternbuch der Kriminologie*, I and II. 1933-6.
S. Ettinger, *Das Verbrecherproblem in anthropologischer und soziologischer Beleuchtung*. 1907.
R. Garofalo, *La criminologia*. 1885. Several later editions. Translated into French and English.
J. L. Gillin, *Criminology and Penology*. 1926.
Fred. E. Haynes, *Criminology*. 1930.
W. Healy and A. F. Bronner, *Delinquents and Criminals: their Making and Unmaking*. 1926.
Ch. R. Henderson, *Introduction of the Dependent, Defective, and Delinquent Classes*. 1909
O. Kinberg, *Basic problems of criminology*. Copenhagen. 1935.
Clyde L. King and others, *Modern Crime: its Prevention and Punishment*. (The Annals of the American Academy of political and social science, CXXV. 1926.)
J. Michael and Mortimer J. Adler, *Crime, Law, and Social Science*. 1933.

[1] For the reader's guidance we mention below some of the literature on the subject, different works of which, in their turn, contain extensive bibliographies.

Messrs. Nijhoff (Den Haag) some time ago published *A systematic list of the principal works of criminal law and criminology* (1909).

A. Macdonald, *Man and abnormal man* (1905), contains an extensive bibliography on criminology.

John H. Wigmore has published *A preliminary bibliography of modern criminal law and criminology* (1909, Chicago), Thorsten Sellin, *A brief guide to penological literature* (1931), and D. C. Culver, *Bibliography of crime and criminal justice* (New York, 1934): very thorough.

About American literature, *vide* the book by A. F. Kuhlman, *A guide to material on crime and criminal justice* (1929, New York), which is, practically speaking, complete.

APPENDIX II

A. Morris, *Criminology*. 1934.
M. Parmelee, *Criminology*. 1918.
C. Bernaldo de Quirós, *Modern theories of criminality*. 1911.
Report on the Causes of Crime, I, II. Report No. 13 of the National Commission on law observance and enforcement (Official American Report). 1931.
J. R. B. de Roos, *Inleiding tot de beoefening der crimineele aetiologie*. 1908.
O. Saldaña, *La criminologie nouvelle*. 1929.
Max G. Schlapp and E. H. Smith, *The New Criminology*. 1928.
G. H. Sutherland, *Criminology*. 1924.
G. Tarde, *La philosophie pénale*. 1890. Several later editions. Translated into English.
L. Vervaeck, *Syllabus du cours d'anthropologie criminelle donné a la prison de Forest*. 1926
W. A. Willemse and C. T. Rademeyer, *Krimonologie*. Pre-. toria. 1933.

B. CRIMINAL ANTHROPOLOGY

a. In a restricted sense

A. Aletrino, *Handleiding bij de studie der crimineele anthropologie*, I and II. 1903-4.
A. Baer, *Der Verbrecher in anthropologischer Beziehung*. 1893.
H. Havelock Ellis, *The Criminal*. 1889. Translated into German in 1895, under the title *Verbrecher und Verbrechen*.
Ch. Goring, *The English Convict*. 1913. An abbreviated edition of this appeared in 1915.
W. Healy, *The Individual Delinquent*. 1915.
J. L. A. Koch, *Die Frage nach dem geborenen Verbrecher*. 1894.
H. Kurella, *Naturgeschichte des Verbrechers*. 1893.
J. Lange, *Verbrechen als Schicksal*. 1929.
A. Lenz, *Grundriss der Kriminalbiologie*. 1927.
C. Lombroso, *L'uomo delinquente*. 1876. Several later editions. Translated into French, English and German.
A. Marro, *I caratteri dei delinquenti*. 1887.

b. Sex[1]

M. R. Fernald, M. H. S. Hayes, and A. Dawley, *A Study of Women Delinquents in New York State*. 1920.
C. Granier, *La femme criminelle*. 1906.
H. Krille, *Weibliche Kriminalität und Ehe*. 1931.
C. Lombroso and G. Ferrero, *La donna delinquente, la prostituta e la donna normale*. 1893. Several later editions. Translated into Franch.
C. Loosjes, *Bijdrage tot de studie van de criminaliteit der vrouw*. 1894.
O. Mönkemöller, *Korrektionsanstalt und Landarmenhaus*. Ein soziologischer Beitrag zur Kriminalität und Psychopathologie des Weibes. 1908.
P. Näcke, *Verbrechen und Wahnsinn beim Weibe*. 1894.
S. Weinberg, *Ueber den Einfluss der Geschlechtsfunktionen auf die weibliche Kriminalität*. 1907.

c. Age

M. G. Barnett, *Young Delinquents*. 1913.
J. Bresler, *Greisenalter und Criminalität*. 1907.
C. Burt, *The Young Delinquent*. 1925, new ed., 1927.
E. A. D E. Carp, *Het misdadige kind in psychologisch opzicht*. 1932.
G. L. Duprat, *La criminalité dans l'adolescence*. 1907.
L. Ferriani, *Minderjährige Verbrecher*. 1896.
L. Gervai, *Kindliche und jugendliche Verbrecher*. 1914.
Sheldon and Eleanor Glueck, *One thousand juvenile delinquents*. 1934.
A. Gregor und E. Voigtländer, *Die Verwahrlosung*. 1918.
H. W. Gruhle, *Die Ursachen der jugendlichen Verwahrlosung und Kriminalität*. 1912.
D. Lund, *Ueber die Ursachen der Jugendasozialität*. 1918.
W. D. Morrison, *Juvenile Offenders*. 1896.
A. Racine, *Les enfants traduits en justice*. 1935
M Raux, *Nos jeunes détenus*. 1890.
J. R. B. de Roos, *De criminaliteit op leeftijden van 70 jaar en hooger*. 1910.

[1] Some of the works mentioned here belong also to C. (criminal sociology), and D. (criminal psychology).

APPENDIX II

C. CRIMINAL SOCIOLOGY

a. General

W. A. Bonger, *Criminalité et conditions économiques*. 1905. American edition published in 1915.
N. Colajanni, *Sociologia criminale*, I, II. 1889.
E. Ferri, *La sociologia criminale*. 1884. Several later editions. Translated into French and English.
E. Joachim, *Konjunktur und Kriminalität*. 1933.
J. van Kan, *Les causés économiques de la criminalité*. 1903.
C. Lombroso, *Le crime. Causes et remèdes*. 1899. Translated into English.
A. Lorulot, *Crime et société*. 1923.
G. von Mayr, *Statistik und Gesellschaftslehre III. Moralstatistik*. 1917, p. 938 et seq.
G. Matteotti, *La recidiva*. 1910.
J. Maxwell, *Le crime et la société*. 1912.
Ad. Quetelet, *Physique sociale II*. 1869.
E. Renger, *Kriminalität, Preis und Lohn*. 1933.
E. Roesner, *Der Einfluss von Wirtschaftslage, Alkohol und Jahreszeit auf die Kriminalität*. 1930.
E. Rozengart, *Le crime comme produit social et économique*. 1929.
D. S. Thomas, *Social Aspects of the Business Cycle*. 1925.

b. Some special subjects
1. Economic criminality

N. Anderson, *The Hobo*. 1923.
E. Florian and G. Cavaglieri, *I vagabondi*. I. 1897. II. 1900.
J. Flynt, *Tramping with Tramps*. 1899.
H. T. de Graaf, *Karakter en behandeling van veroordeelden wegens landlooperij*. 1914.
R. Heindl, *Der Berufsverbrecher*. 1926.
A. John, *Die Rückfallsdiebe*. 1929.
R. Laschi, *Le crime financier*. 1901.
Marie et P. Meunier, *Les Vagabonds*. 1908.
N. Manzini, *Le varie specie di furto*, 2nd ed. 1913.
N. Müller, *Biografisch aetiologisch onderzoek over recidive bij misdadigers tegen den eigendom*. 1908.
A. Pagnier, *Le Vagabond*. 1910.

H. Weiss. *Die Hehler.* 1930.
H. Trommer, *Urkundenfalschung und Betrug im Weltkriege.* 1928.

2. Sexual criminality

A. G. Hess, *Die Kinderschändung.* 1934.
J. R. B. de Roos, *De sexueele criminaliteit.* 1909.
E. Wulffen, *Der Sexualverbrecher.* 1910.

3. Aggressive criminality

H. C. Brearly, *Homicide in the United States.* 1932.
E. Ferri, *L'omicidio.* 1894. New edition in 1925, under the title *L'omicida.*
P. Gast, *Die Mörder.* 1930.
L. Holtz, *Les Crimes passionnels.* 1904.
W. Lorentz, *Die Todschläger.* 1932.
L. Proal, *Le crime et le suicide passionnels.* 1900.
E. Ristow, *Die Kriminalität der Roheitsdelikte.* 1933.

4. Political criminality

G. Angiolella, *Delitti e delinquenti politici.* 1903.
E. J. Gumbel, *Vier Jahre politischer Mord.* 1922.
C. Lombroso and R. Laschi, *Il delitto politico e le revoluzioni.* 1890. Several later editions. Translated into French and German.
C. Lombroso, *Gli anarchici.* 1894. Several later editions. Translated into French.
E. Régis, *Les Régicides dans l'histoire et dans le présent.* 1890.

c. Criminality in various countries

Criminaliteit in Amsterdam en van Amsterdammers. Statistische Mededeelingen door het Bureau van Statistiek der Gemeente, Amsterdam. 1932.
F. Ammoun, *La Syrie criminelle.* 1929.
Die Kriminalität im Kanton Bern, 1924–29. Mitteilungen des Statistischen Bureaus des Kantons Bern. 1932.
W. A. Bonger, *De criminaliteit van Nederland.* (Mensch en Maatschappij, VI. 1930.)

APPENDIX II

A. Bournet, *De la criminalité en France et en Italie*. 1884.
E. Fornasari di Verce, *La criminalità e le vicende economiche d'Italia dal 1873 al 1890*. 1894.
H. Guégo *Contribution à l'étude statistique sur la criminalité en France de 1826 à 1900*. 1902.
H. Herz, *Verbrechen und Verbrechertum in Oesterreich*. 1908.
C. Jacquart, *La criminalité belge 1868–1909*. 1912.
M. L. Kolaly, *Essai sur les causes de la criminalité actuelle en Egypte*. 1929.
A. Meyer, *Die Verbrechen in ihrem Zusammenhang mit den wirtschaftlichen und socialen Verhältnissen im Kanton Zürich*. 1895.
W. Starke, *Verbrechen und Verbrecher in Preussen 1854–78*. 1884.
A. Wadler, *Die Verbrechensbewegung im östlichen Europa. I. Die Kriminalität der Balkanländer*. 1908.

D. Criminal Psychology

a. Psychology of the criminal in general

P. Despine, *Psychologie naturelle*, II, III. 1868.
J. V. van Dijck, *Bijdragen tot de psychologie van den misdadiger*. 1906.
G. H. A. Feber, *Beschouwingen over crimineele psychologie*. 1934.
R. H. Gault, *Criminology*. 1932.
M. H. Göring, *Kriminalpsychologie*. 1922.
W. Healy, *The Individual Delinquent*. 1915.
W. Healy, *Mental Conflicts and Misconduct*. 1926.
B. Hollander, *The Psychology of Misconduct, Vice, and Crime*. 1922.
M. Kauffmann, *Die Psychologie des Verbrechens*. 1912.
C. Murchison, *Criminal Intelligence*. 1926.
G. W. Pailthorpe, *What We Put in Prison*. 1932.
W. T. Root, Jr., *A psychological and educational survey of 1916 prisoners in the Western Penitentiary of Pennsylvania*. 1926.
M. Hamblin Smith, *The Psychology of the Criminal*. 1923.
Sheldon and Eleanor T. Glueck, *500 Criminal Careers*. 1930.
H. Többen, *Neuere Beobachtungen über die Psychologie der zu*

lebenslänglicher Zuchthausstrafe verurteilten oder begnadigten Verbrecher. 1927.
W. A. Willemse, *Constitution types in delinquency.* 1932.
E. Wulffen, *Psychologie des Verbrechers.* 1908. In 1926, under the title *Kriminalpsychologie.*

b. Psychology of some classes of criminals

1. Economic criminals

A. Anderson, *The Hobo.* 1923.
J. Flynt, *Tramping with Tramps.* 1899.
E. Florian and G. Cavaglieri, *I vagabondi.* I, 1897. II, 1900.
H. T. de Graaf, *Karakter en behandeling van veroordeelden wegens landlooperij.* 1914.
Dr. Marie et B. Meunier, *Les vagabonds.* 1908.
A. Pagnier, *Le vagabond.* 1910.
K. Willmans, *Zur Psychopathologie des Landstreichers.* 1906.
R. Heindl, *Der Berufsverbrecher.* 1926.
V. Manzini, *Le varie specie di furto.* 2nd edition, 1913.
E. Michon, *Un peu de l'âme des bandits.* Undated; probably 1913.
N. Muller, *Biografisch-aetiologisch onderzoek over recidive bij misdadigers tegen den eigendom.* 1908.
R. Laschi, *Le crime financier.* 1901.
W. A. Pannenborg, *Bijdrage tot de psychologie van den misdadiger, in het bijzonder van den brandstichter.* 1912.[1]
H. Többen, *Beiträge zur Psychologie und Psychopathologie der Brandstifter.* 1917.

2. Sexual criminals

E. Wulffen, *Der Sexualverbrecher.* 1910.

3. Aggressive criminals

A. Bjerre, *Zur Psychologie des Mordes.* 1925.
E. Ferri, *L'omicidio.* 1894. New edition in 1925 under the title *L'omicida.*
R. Gaupp, *Zur Psychologie des Massenmordes.* 1914.
R. L. Holtz, *Les crimes passionnels.* 1904.

---

[1] This work should also be listed under 3, *Aggressive Criminals.*

F. von Holzendorff, *Die Psychologie des Mordes*.
A. Wetzel and K. Wilmanns, *Geliebtenmörder*. 1913.

4. Political criminals

C. Lombroso and R. Laschi, *Il delitto politico e le revoluzione*. 1890.
C. Lombroso, *Gli anarchici*. 1894.
E. Régis, *Les régicides dans l'histoire et dans le présent*. 1890.

5. Collective criminality

G. le Bon, *Psychologie des foules*. 1895. Numerous later editions. Translated into various languages.
W. von Bechterew, *Die Bedeutung der Suggestion im sozialen Leben*. 1905.
H. van der Hoeven, *Psychiatrie III*. Chapter XXIV, 2nd edition. 1930.
E. Höpler und P. Schilder, *Suggestion und Strafrechtswissenschaft*. 1926.
S. Sighele, *La folla delinquente*. 1892. Translated into French and Dutch.
S. Sighele, *Psychologie des sectes*. 1898.
G. Tarde, *Les crimes des foules. Foules et sectes, au point de vue criminel* (both these in *Essais et mélanges sociologiques*. 1895.)

c. Psychology of witnesses' evidence

F. Gorphe, *La critique du témoignage*. 1924. 2nd edition, 1927.
O. Mönkemöller, *Psychologie und Psychopathologie der Aussage*. 1930.
H. Münsterberg, *On the Witness Stand*. 1925.
P. Plaut, *Der Zeuge und seine Aussage im Strafprozess*. 1931.
W. Stern, *Jugendliche Zeugen in Sittlichkeitsprozessen*. 1926.

INDEX

Aletrino, A, 60, 70, 140
Aristotle, 27, 155
Aschaffenburg, G., 107, 111, 117, 142
Antheaume, A., 95
Antonini, G., 26, 30
Aubry, P., 81
Avé-Lallemant, F. C. B., 139

Bacon, F., 1
Baer, A., 68, 69, 81, 96, 141
Baernreither, J. M., 84
Baets, M. de, 127
Balzac, H. de, 17
Barnes, H. E., 60
Bataille, A., 16
Battaglia, B., 83
Bebel, A., 83
Beccaria, C., 32, 34
Bemmelen, J. M. van, 38
Benedikt, M., 66, 79
Bentham, J., 32, 35, 38
Berends, 70, 71
Birnbaum, K., 8
Bleuler, E., 59
Bodin, J., 106
Boerhaave, 36
Bonger, W. A., 26, 55, 63, 91, 95, 96, 98, 100, 102–5, 128, 130, 132–4
Bournet, A., 81
Bower, L. F., 6
Brissot de Warville, J. P., 32, 34
Broca, P, 45, 56
Brusse, J. M., 88
Buckle, H. Th., 107
Burt, C., 85, 147

Cabanis, P. J. G., 46
Calkoen, H., 36
Calvert, E. Roy, 40, 113
Calvin, 30
Carus, C. G., 30, 56
Casper, J. L., 58
Charpentier, R., 96

Colajanni, N., 82
Comte, A., 19, 47
Condorcet, A. de, 47–8
Corre, A., 27, 141

Dally, E., 57
Darwin, Ch., 58
Davenant, Ch., 48
Democritus, 21
Despine, P., 18, 58, 139, 142, 149
Dresel, E. G., 98
Dreyfus, G. L., 145
Dubuisson, P., 95
Ducpétiaux, Ed., 53
Dumont, E., 32
Dÿck, J. V. van, 70, 145

Ellis, Havelock, 26, 59, 132, 136
Enfantin, B. P., 44
Engels, F., 42
Erasmus, 30
Esquirol, J. E. D., 45, 57, 138
Exner, F., 105

Faure, 16
Ferguson, A., 107
Ferrero, G., 59
Ferri, E., 17, 35, 59, 76–7, 107, 114–5, 117–9, 123, 132
Feuerbach, A. von, 15, 138
Filangieri, G., 32
Fischer, A., 64
Fornasari di Verce, E., 77
Fourier, Ch., 44
Fourier, J., 49
Fraenkel, M. O., 60
Francotte, X., 58
Francken, C. J. Wijnaendts, 22
Frederiks, K. J., 46
Fry, E., 38
Fuchs, V., 31–2

Gaedeken, P., 107
Gall, F. J., 36, 45, 56, 138
Galton, F., 122

175

INDEX

Gardikas, C. G., 27
Garofalo, R., 59
Gaupp, R., 145
Gauss, K. F., 121
Goethe, 6, 12
Godwin, W., 42-3
Goring, Ch., 72, 147
Göring, M. H., 145
Graaf, H. T. de, 96, 136, 146
Grant, J., 48
Grataroli, G., 30
Gregor, G., 84
Grönlund, O., 106
Gross, H., 81, 141-3
Gruhle, H. W., 84, 87, 144, 145
Guenther, L., 31
Guerry, A. M., 50

Hall, Ch. 42-3
Halley, E., 48
Hamel, G. A. van, 117
Hamel, J. A, van, 35
Häring, 15, 137
Healy, W., 60, 146
Heindl, R., 9, 142
Hentig, H. von, 37
Herder, 107
Herodotus, 106
Hesse, R., 17
Heymans, G., 18, 21, 136, 145
Hillesum, H., 16
Hippocrates, 106
Hirsch, P., 83
Hitzig, 15, 136
Hobhouse, L. T., 63
Hodgskin, Th., 43
Hoeven, H. van der, 8
Holbach, D', 34
Hollander, B., 147
Horsley, J, W., 132
Howard, J., 33
Hume, D., 21, 24, 29, 47, 107

Jaeger, J., 127
Jelgersma, G., 67
John, V., 48
Joly, H., 127, 132

Kafka, G., 145
Kan, J. van, 26-7, 30, 55

Kaufmann, M., 144
King, C., 48
Kovalewsky, P., 140
Krauss, A., 141
Krauss, F. A. K., 127
Kretschmer, E., 74
Kruyswyck-Hamburger, R.C. S., 90
Kulischer, 63
Kurella, H., 59, 140

Lacassagne, A., 78-9, 82, 95, 107
Lafargue, P., 83
Lamarck, J., 58, 78
Laplace, P. S. de, 49
Laschi, R., 59, 115
Laurent, E., 81, 132, 142
Lauvergne, H., 56, 138
Lavater, J. K., 37
Leibnitz, 21
Lenz, A., 59
Ley, A., 96
Liepmann, M., 105
Lindenau, 9
Linguet, S. N. H., 34
Lilienthal, K. von, 144
Liszt, F. von, 107, 116-7
Locard, E., 9
Loewe, A., 92
Lombroso, C., 58, 60-76, 78-9, 115, 118, 140, 147
Lotin, J., 50
Lucas, P., 57
Lund, D., 87
Luther, 30

Mably, G. B. de, 34
Malthus, R., 34
Magnan, 79
Manouvrier, L., 61, 66, 68-9, 71, 75, 79, 119
Manulescu, 17
Marat, J. P., 31, 34
Marro, 26, 30, 37, 58-9, 140
Marx, K., 81-2
Masmonteil, G., 31
Maudsley, H., 57
Maunier, R., 46
Mayr, G. von, 54-5, 91
Mesdag, S., van, 17, 45

INDEX

Meslier, J., 34
Mettrie, J. O. de la, 36
Meyers, S. J., 16
Montesquieu, 31, 33-4, 47, 106-7
More, Th., 26, 28-9
Moreau, G., 16
Moreau-Christophe, L. M., 54, 56
Morel, A. B., 57, 68, 138
Morelli, 34
Morrison, W. D., 85
Muller, N., 16-7, 132, 146
Mueller-Lyer, F., 6
Murchison, C., 147

Naecke, P., 69, 81
Napoleon, 46
Newton, 121
Niceforo, A., 9
Nicolson, D., 58
Nissl, F., 144
Noorduyn, J. P. F. A., 86

Oettingen, A. von, 54, 127
Ottolenghi, 67
Overbeck, A. von, 31
Owen, R. 43
Oyens, J. C. de Marez, 133

Pailthorpe, G. W. 147
Pannenborg, W. A., 146
Pasteur, L., 78
Paulsen, F., 135
Pestalozzi, H., 35
Petty, W., 48
Phelps, H. A., 91
Pinel, Ph., 44, 56, 138
Pitaval, F. G. de, 15, 136, 139
Plato, 27
Pollitz, P., 32, 143
Porta, G. B. Della, 30
Prichard, J. C., 57, 138
Prins, Ad., 117
Proal, L., 127

Quack, H. P. G., 34, 42-3
Quetelet, Ad., 49, 50, 52, 107, 121-123
Quiros, C. B. de, 60

Rameckers, J. M., 35
Ratzel, F., 107
Raux. M., 81, 84
Régis, E., 81
Reiss, 9
Richer, F., 137
Roesner, E., 54, 91, 107, 109, 112
Romilly, S., 38
Roos, J. R. B. de, 105
Root, Jr., W. T., 147
Rousseau, J., 7, 31, 33
Ruggles-Brise, E., 41

Saint-Hilaire, E. Geoffroy, 58, 78
Saint-Simon, C. H. de, 47
Schaumann, J. C. G., 138
Schenk, W., 17
Schlapp, M. G., 6
Schneickert, H., 9, 31
Scholz, W. von, 138
Schopenhauer, 21
Schott, S., 144
Schreyvogl, F., 28
Shakespeare, 137
Sighele, S., 59, 140
Simons, D., 8, 117
Sinclair, J., 48
Smith, Ad., 47
Smith, E. H., 6
Smith, M. Hamblin, 147
Solnar, 106
Sommer, R., 59, 143
Soquet, J., 81
Soudek, J., 91
Spann, O., 86
Spencer, H., 86
Spielmeyer, 69
Spinoza, 21
Spuerzheim, G., 45, 56, 138
Steinmetz, S. R., 62-3
Strabo, 106
Stursberg, H., 127
Suermondt, M. G. L., 89, 105
Süssmilch, J. P., 48

Taine, H., 107
Tarde, G., 78, 80, 112
Thomas, D. S., 91

Thomas Aquinas, 28
Thompson, J. B., 58
Thompson, W., 43
Thót, L. von., 60
Toennies, F., 85
Topinard, P., 1
Trommer, H., 94
Turati, F., 82
Turgot, 47, 107

Virgilio, G., 58
Voigtländer, G., 85
Voltaire, 31, 47
Vries, H. de, 122

Wallace, R., 34
Wetzel, A., 144-5

Wichmann, C. G., 31
Wiersma, E. D., 136
Willenbuecher, F., 32
Wilmanns, K., 144-5
Winkler, C., 59, 61, 70, 71, 119
Woude, Th. van der, 96, 98, 100
Woytinski, W., 91-2
Wulffen, E., 117, 143

Yocas, P., 106
Young, A., 48

Zeno, 23
Zola, E., 17

PRINTED BY
JARROLD AND SONS LTD.
NORWICH